Burr, Clinton and the *Falls* of General Benjamin Hovey

KARL CONNELL

© 2013, Karl Connell

All rights reserved.

No part of this book may be utilized in any form by, any means, including, without limitation, photocopying, recording, or any information or retrieval system without the permission in writing from Wintoon Waters, c/o Karl Connell, Jr., 112 Bentley Village Court, Naples, FL 34110-8082.

ISBN: 978-1-60414-708-7

PUBLISHED BY:
Fideli Publishing Inc.
www.FideliPublishing.com

Cover design by Barbara Gunia, cover art by Laura Brock.

For Two Gioias
And one Ladd

Other Works by Karl Connell

Financing a Theatrical Production, Act II,
    Federal Legal Publications, 1964.

Wintoon,
    Privately Published, 1993.

Tularosa,
    Privately Published, 1998.

Biography of an Inventor, Dr. Karl Connell,
    Wintoon Waters, 2008.

PREFACE

When challenged to name the Founding Fathers of the United States of America, most of us would mention the first three Presidents, George Washington, John Adams and Thomas Jefferson, then maybe recall that canny old kite flier, Benjamin Franklin. Some might throw in Madison, the fourth President for good measure. The eminent historian, Richard B. Morris, who wrote *Seven who Shaped Our Destiny*, included these five and also Alexander Hamilton and John Jay, even though Jay declined an opportunity to sign the Declaration of Independence. Some might also include Aaron Burr, the third Vice President, or George Clinton, the fourth and fifth Vice President.

These "Founders" had considerable education. Five were Ivy League: Adams went to Harvard; Burr and Madison to Princeton; and Hamilton and Jay to Columbia. Of those remaining, Jefferson attended William & Mary, Washington had a limited amount of private tutoring, Franklin was self-taught at the printing trade and Clinton studied law.

On the other hand, not one of these Founders answered the call of Paul Revere. None of them joined a simple blacksmith in Worcester, Massachusetts, in defying English rule and closing the Courts that governed Massachusetts in 1774. It was the minutemen of Massachusetts who answered that call and the action of a blacksmith and the body of plain folk who supported men like him throughout the colonies that inspired the Continental Congress to declare Independence.[1] This book is about one such person, a minuteman. He did not write the Declaration of Independence or contribute Articles to the Constitution, but, in addition to service as a minuteman, he participated in founding a religious society, a town, an academy, a county and a canal company. He also had his failures. His name is Benjamin Hovey. Although unique, his story represents many of the challenges and opportunities of Revolutionary times.

He became acquainted, indeed involved with two early candidates for president, Aaron Burr and George Clinton. The characters of Burr and Clinton are reflected by their disparate treatment of Hovey.

All the principal events in this story are based on historical records, except as otherwise noted. The connection of these events, however, such as the trip by Hovey's family from Oxford, Massachusetts, to Oxford, New York, is based on records of similar events at the time.

INTRODUCTION

My father, Dr. Karl Connell, attained a touch of renown as a Major for having developed the American gas mask in World War I. His exciting life is set forth in my first biography, *Biography of an Inventor, Dr. Karl Connell.* My mother may have been a little jealous of his renown for she often mentioned her minuteman great-grandfather Benjamin Hovey, who became a General. Accordingly, following the biblical commandment to honor thy father and thy mother, four years ago I set out to find the place of my great-great-grandfather in history. There was little to go on, three pages in *The Annals of Oxford* (New York) and a page in *The Hovey Book*. But as the footnotes will show, in the last four years with the help of many talented researchers lauded in the appended Acknowledgements, I have unearthed enough to tell a story — a story which I believe illustrates that in three vital respects not much has changed since 1776.

First, the majority of people prefer the safe harbor of working for others, often for large corporations or the government, on well-traveled roads to security; others are willing to take risks and innovate. Some succeed spectacularly like Steve Jobs or Mark Zuckerberg and his associates. Many more try, but often fail.

Second, today in these United States, the same battle rages over the power of the federal government versus the power of each of the fifty states as it did at the ratification of the Constitution. The Supreme Court has recently decided that the power of Congress is limited — it cannot use the Constitution's Commerce clause to force a citizen to sign a contract against his will, thus deferring to the states. It further decided that the power of the federal government to tax can be used to force a citizen to pay for the operation of hospital emergency rooms even if he or she never uses them.

Third, today some, indeed many, politicians and other leaders attain their position of power by using people for a particular purpose and abandoning them when that purpose has been attained. Others are loyal and steadfast in support of their subordinates to the very end. You may find a striking example of the latter type in the support of Benjamin Hovey by George Clinton and of the former type in the withdrawal of support by Aaron Burr.

Among other family legends, one of his grandsons[2] claimed Benjamin Hovey was the first man to answer the call of Paul Revere. The recent and exhaustively researched book, *Paul Revere's Ride,* by David Hackett Fischer, states that the first man has never been identified. On April 18 1775, Revere was rowed across the Charles River from Boston to Charlestown. To pass silently below the towering stern of a British ship of the line, HMS Somerset, the oarsmen are alleged to have muffled their oars with a woman's woolen undergarment, hastily flung to them, still warm from her body, out of an upstairs window just before they embarked. At Charlestown, as Revere was "preparing to travel west to Lexington, arrangements were made for another 'express' rider to gallop north with the news that [the British were coming by sea] he had brought from Boston. The identity of the other courier is not known. Many people heard him in the dark but few actually saw him. He set out from Charlestown at about the same hour as Paul Revere himself. His route took him north through the present towns of Medford, Winchester, Woburn and Wilmington. So swiftly did he gallop on dark and dangerous roads that by two o'clock in the morning he was in the town of Tewksbury on the Merrimack River, twenty-five miles north of Boston.

"Whoever he may have been, the messenger knew exactly where he was going and what he was to do. When he reached Tewksbury, he spurred his horse through the streets of the sleeping village, and rode directly to the farm of Captain John Trull on Stickney Hill, near the town's training field. Captain Trull was the head of the Tewksbury militia, and a pivotal figure in the alarm system that Whig leaders had organized during the last few months. He was awakened by the courier who told him, 'I have alarmed all the towns from Charlestown to here.'"[3]

Could the unnamed courier have been Benjamin Hovey? On April 18, 1775, the date the ride commenced, he was 17 years, one month and five days old. While he was born and grew up in Sutton, now part of Oxford, Massachusetts, some 50-odd miles from Boston, Tewksbury is only about 10 miles from Boxford where his Mother's family lived. He could have planned to stay with that family. We will explore and confirm or explode that family legend.

His great regret in life was that he had no formal education. Thus, unlike the biographies of John Adams, who left us with thousands of letters, George Washington, who had his letters copied, and the other well-known founders, whose biographies are encapsulated in the Appendix under Cast of Characters, his life is sparsely documented. An extensive "Memorial," more like a lawyer's brief, was printed at his behest and submitted to a committee of the Senate in support of a projected canal around the falls in the Ohio River. Only one of his letters could be found. There are a number of existing public recollections and stories, however, about this athletic, vigorous and pioneering character and the exciting times in which he lived.

TABLE OF CONTENTS

Preface .... *vii*
Introduction .... *ix*
List of Illustrations .... *xiv*
Appendix .... *xv*

CHAPTER ONE	Burr, Clinton and Hovey	1
CHAPTER TWO	The Massachusetts Bay Colony	7
CHAPTER THREE	The Tories and the Whigs	17
CHAPTER FOUR	Seventeen Seventy Five	25
CHAPTER FIVE	The Founding of Universalism	39
CHAPTER SIX	Governor Clinton	49
CHAPTER SEVEN	The Road to Fort Hill	59
CHAPTER EIGHT	Founding Oxford, New York	81
CHAPTER NINE	Hovey's Settlement	91
CHAPTER TEN	Founding the Oxford Academy	97
CHAPTER ELEVEN	Founding Chenango County	103
CHAPTER TWELVE	Convicted by Court Martial	113
CHAPTER THIRTEEN	Promoted to General	119
CHAPTER FOURTEEN	Founding the Canal Company	127
CHAPTER FIFTEEN	Failure at the Falls	143
CHAPTER SIXTEEN	Canal Mania	151
EPILOGUE	Trial, Exile and Tragedy	159

LIST OF ILLUSTRATIONS

Map of Massachusetts Bay Colony xvi
The 1668 Hovey House... 10
King George III 16
Paul Revere 27
Old Nel Whinnied.. 30
General George Washington 35
George Clinton 48
Daniel Shays and Job Shattuck 61
Melancton Smith.. 78
General Marinus Willett... 79
Map of Present Day Township of Oxford..................................... 90
Illustration of Early Oxford 93
James Glover 101
Alphena Hovey Glover 102
Benjamin Hovey 104
Map of Chenango County.. 105
Aaron Burr 107
Thomas Jefferson 112
Early Map of Ohio River Falls 129
Burr fatally wounds Hamilton in Duel 131
James Wilkinson.. 133
George Rogers Clark cabin 140
Harman Blennerhassett mansion 142
Washington's Patomack Company logo and Barge scene 150
Aaron Burr late in life 158

APPENDIX

I. Chapter Notes 165
II. Acknowledgements 173
III. Bibliography 177
IV. Chronology 181
V. Cast of Characters 187
        John Adams 187
        Aaron Burr 187
        George Clinton 187
        Benjamin Franklin 188
        Alexander Hamilton 188
        John Jay 188
        Thomas Jefferson 188
        James Kent 189
        James Madison 189
        James Monroe 189
        Melancton Smith 189
        George Washington 189
        James Wilkinson 190
        Marinus Willett 190
VI. Index 191

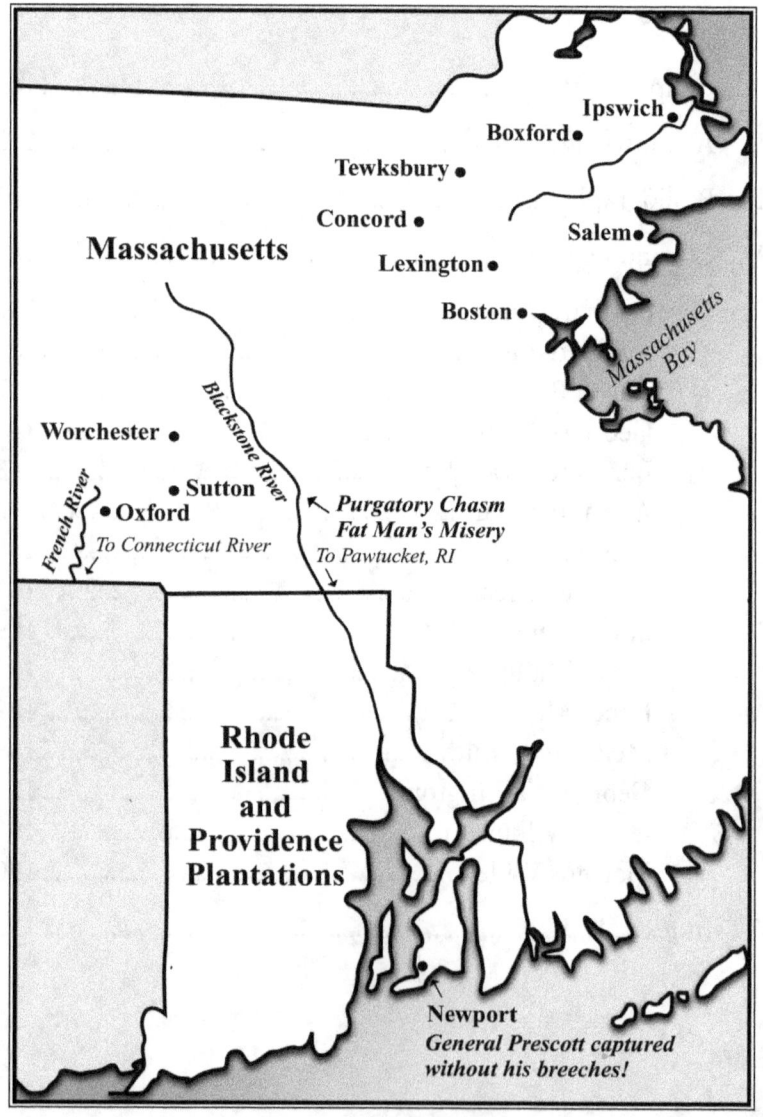

Map of Massachusetts Bay Colony

CHAPTER ONE

Burr, Clinton and Hovey

As different as they could be

Aaron Burr, George Clinton and Benjamin Hovey were three men of very different backgrounds, each of whom served the cause of freedom during the Revolution that founded the United States of America.

The eldest, George Clinton was elected Governor of New York State shortly after its first Constitution was adopted in Kingston in 1777, and served six consecutive three-year terms until June 30, 1795, and a seventh from July 1, 1801, to August 30, 1804. His accomplishments as wartime and peacetime governor are remarkable. As wartime governor he also served as head of the New York Militia. He succeeded in turning back the British attempt to come up the Hudson to Albany, defending the frontier and stopping mutinies. In addition, he helped supply the Continental Army under Washington.

As governor he was most vexed by the two northeastern counties that wanted to form the Republic of Vermont, a battle he eventually lost. The many loyalists in New York were also a problem. The governor enforced laws confiscating their property, laws in some cases that he did not personally favor. He made many grants of lands acquired by treaty or force from Native American tribes. Later he allowed his name to be advanced for president, ran for president, and served twice as Vice President during Thomas Jefferson's second term and James Madison's first. He is, however, not as well-known as he should be. Records of his early accomplishments were destroyed when the British burned Kingston, then New York's capital, in 1777 and later records were destroyed in the New York Library fire of 1911.[4]

We do know a great deal about Aaron Burr, soldier, New York lawyer, Assemblyman, Attorney General, U. S. Senator, Assemblyman again, and then Vice President during Jefferson's first term. There are said to be more than 200 books and articles, many concerning his duel with Alexander Hamilton or trial for treason.[5] Burr had an exceptional education for that day. Burr's father was the President of the College of New Jersey (now Princeton), and his mother was a daughter of the distinguished cleric, Jonathan Edwards. Both parents died before he was four. He was raised by his uncle, Timothy Edwards, in Elizabethtown, New Jersey. Uncle Timothy was such a severe disciplinarian that Burr tried to run away from home several times.

Extremely bright, he was tutored at home and applied to enter Princeton when he was only eleven. He was so small in stature that he looked younger than his age and, therefore, was rejected. When he was thirteen he applied again to the Junior Class but was accepted as a sophomore. He graduated in 1772. The next year he briefly studied religion. Finding it did not suit him, he turned to the study of law in Litchfield, Massachusetts. Soon he left to join the Continental Army surrounding Boston, Massachusetts and volunteered to go on the ill-conceived trek through the wilderness of northern Maine to assault Quebec. There he was beside General Richard Montgomery when Montgomery was killed, leading to the failure to take Quebec. After distinguished service in the Continental Army and promotion to Lieutenant Colonel, in March 1779 Burr resigned from service pleading ill health.[6]

In August 1778 he had met Theodosia Bartow Prevost on a five day trip down the Hudson River. She was a brilliant, cultivated woman, ten years his senior married to an English officer and mother of five children. Her husband was serving in Georgia and later in Jamaica where he died in October 1781. On July 2, 1782, Aaron Burr married Theodosia Prevost, One wonders if she not only served as his wife, but also fulfilled the role of the mother he never knew. In June 1783, they had a daughter, also named Theodosia.

Aaron Burr was admitted to the New York Bar and they first settled in Albany but moved to New York City in 1783 as the British finally left that city. There he practiced law, was elected to the New York State Assembly, serving there in 1784 and 1785. He was appointed Attorney General of New York State by Governor George Clinton in 1789 and served in that office until November 1791. While still Attorney General he was elected United States Senator with the strong backing of New York City's Tammany Hall and served in Congress from March 1791 until March 3, 1797. Tragically his wife died of cancer on May 18, 1794. Burr devoted much energy to the education of his daughter. He made every effort to make her fluent in both English and French and conversant with the leading authors in both languages.

The scant historical records concerning Benjamin Hovey are cited in the Chapter Notes at the end of this book. We do not know when Benjamin Hovey first met George Clinton, 19, or Aaron Burr, two years his senior, but both George Clinton, as Governor, and Aaron Burr, as Attorney General, were serving on the Appointments Committee in 1790 when the Committee appointed Hovey to be a Major in the New York Militia.[7] We also know that Burr and Hovey together served in the New York Assembly in 1798. When Hovey was elected by Tioga County, he entered a world of politicians seeking the advantages of power, a world that he could scarcely have imagined as an uneducated youth from the small town of Oxford, Massachusetts.

When Hovey joined the Assembly, he must have been impressed by Albany, then the sixth largest city in the United States. It had become the official capital of New York only the year before, and a new State Hall was being built for meetings of the legislature.[8] He also must have been impressed and surprised by being greeted cordially by Aaron Burr, because Burr had voted against his being seated as an assemblyman from Tioga County in the previous session.

Hovey learned from this defeat; he had to supplement his appeal as a candidate who would bring a new county to his constituents with humor. In those days ethnic jokes were politically correct and frequently told. He doubtless had several about the Praying Nipmugs near his original home in Oxford, Massachusetts — even their name was funny! Also barnyard humor was then in vogue. Having the rival politician stand on a mound in the barnyard to announce his platform and then observe he was standing on a platform of manure was always good for a laugh. He also entertained a lot. This led to his election in 1798.

Aaron Burr likely congratulated Hovey on his success and invited him, along with several other prominent Assemblymen to join him for an evening at Cartwright's Tavern. This no doubt led to an invitation to visit him at Richmond Hill, his estate in New York City. The city was only an overnight trip from Albany.[9] A road down the West Bank of the Hudson River reached Catskill, thence a ferry across to Hudson and on to New York City.[10]

Burr first had been to Richmond Hill when, as a Lieutenant, he was an aide to George Washington during Washington's brief stay there in August 1776 after his defeat by General Howe in Long Island. Burr had adopted an extravagant lifestyle. His first wife died shortly after the birth of their daughter, Theodosia. Burr took a great interest in her education and their social status by acquiring the magnificent estate named Richmond Hill in 1793. It had been built in 1760 by Sir Abraham Mortimer, Commissary of the British Army, on the island named Manhattan, a mile north of New York City, as it was then constituted. It encompassed 160 acres where Greenwich Village now stands. It had previously been occupied by John Adams, while he was Vice President. Enhanced by views of sailing ships constantly passing in the Hudson River, Adams' wife Abigail described it in these glowing terms in a letter to a friend:

"We are delightfully situated ... The prospect all around is beautiful to the highest degree. ... On one side we see a view of the City and of Long Island. The River in front, Jersey and the adjacent country on the other side. You turn a little from the road and enter a gate. A winding road with trees in clumps leads to the house, and all around the house it looks wild and rural as uncultivated nature. . . . You can enter under a piazza into a hall and turning to the right hand ascend a staircase which lands in another of equal dimensions of which I make a drawing room. It has a glass door which opens onto a gallery the whole front of the house which is exceeding pleasant. ... There is upon the back of the house a garden of much greater extent than our Braintree garden, but it is wholly for a walk and flowers. It has a hawthorne (sic) hedge and rows of trees with a broad gravel walk."

During Burr's residency, Richmond Hill was lavishly furnished with such rarities for those days as a large bathtub and a harp and piano-forte. There were also in-laid card tables from the shop of Marinus Willett, a noted cabinet maker and sheriff, later mayor of the City. Besides the gardens, there were stables, with horses to groom and carriages to polish. It took a staff of at least eight to manage the estate. Visitors were treated not only to music, but also lavish meals often featuring oysters, oyster patties, oyster box stew and oysters Algonquin, among other dishes from the nearby beds of shellfish in New York Bay.[11] On Hovey's visits he met many of Burr's friends, including Melancton Smith and Jonathon Lawrence, well-known merchants and politicians and General John Lamb. Burr and Lamb had served together on the unsuccessful attempt to capture Quebec in 1775 and 1776. At the time Hovey met him, General Lamb was the Custom's Collector of the Port of New York, having been appointed in 1784 by the Congress of the Confederation during the Revolution.

Hovey could not but wonder at the different lifestyles of Burr and New York's long-time Governor George Clinton, whom he had known, trusted and respected for some years. Despite their close business relationship and respect for each other, Clinton had never entertained Hovey like Burr.

CHAPTER TWO

The Massachusetts Bay Colony

Five-Pound Passage

Benjamin Hovey's accession to the friendship of such political leaders as future Vice Presidents Aaron Burr and George Clinton seemed highly unlikely at the time of his birth on March 12, 1758. He was born in Sutton, Massachusetts. He was the eighth child of a Daniel Hovey, the great-grandson of the first Hovey to come to New England, also named Daniel Hovey. This original Hovey arrived on the Beagle in 1634, when the customary fare for passage and food for the estimated 60-day western voyage from England was five pounds. He came as part of a group of Puritans, sailing with a fleet of 17 ships into the Charles River. Unlike the Pilgrims, who had broken with the Church of England, the Puritans wanted to remain with the church, but purify and reform it by eliminating the ritual and hierarchy associated with Roman Catholicism. Although the first Daniel Hovey to cross the Atlantic may have been motivated by dissatisfaction with the Church of England, given his youthfulness (only 17 years old), he may have been more highly motivated by adventure and economic opportunity.

The Puritans anchored in the Charles River and founded the City of Boston. Like the Pilgrims, who had settled at Plymouth in 1620, these early immigrants were able to take advantage of abandoned Indian village sites and use deserted fields formerly used for planting corn, beans and squashes. The New England coast had been occupied by many tribes of Native Americans. These tribes included the Wampanoag and the neighboring tribes that spoke the same (Massachusett) language. These were the Natick, Pokanoket, Chappaquiddick and Massachusett. Down the northeastern coast were the Narragansett, Sononce, sometimes called the Pawtucket, Podunk and Mohegan. Further up the northeastern coast were the Penacook, Passamaquoddy and Penobscot.

These coastal tribes had enjoyed a rich and nutritious diet. There were shell fish, mussels, clams and oysters, the latter being rich in iron, calcium, selenium and zinc, so vital for the reproductive health of the native population. There were also fish from the sea, salmon from the streams, occasional waterfowl from the air and deer and small game from the land. There were also nuts and maple syrup from trees, leeks and berries from bogs, honey from hives and eggs from nests. To provide for the long New England winters, these tribes cleared land and cultivated corn, fertilized with fish carcasses. Beans climbed the corn stalks and restored nitrogen to the soil depleted by the corn.

Some early Missionaries, who felt idleness was ungodliness, were dismayed that the Native Americans, particularly the males, had the leisure to enjoy life and, in lieu of toil, the sport of hunting and fishing. Others, such as the Jesuit Priest, Paul le Jeune, in Canada found "our savages are happy, for the two tyrants that provide hell and torture for many of our Europeans, do no reign in their great forests, — I mean ambition and avarice. As they have neither political organization, nor offices, nor dignities, nor any authority, for they only obey their chief through good will toward him, therefore they never kill each other to acquire these honors. Also as they are contented with mere living, not one of them gives himself to the Devil to acquire wealth."

By the time the Pilgrims and Puritans arrived, however, these tribes had been decimated by earlier contact with sailors, fishermen and fur traders from France, England, Portugal and other European nations. These Europeans brought clothing, baskets, beads, rum, guns and gunpowder to trade for furs and corn. They also brought smallpox, influenza, measles, tuberculosis and other diseases to which the natives had little or no immunity. In addition to these diseases, the bubonic plague that peaked in London from 1616 to 1619, also was brought to America and left the coastal areas of New England with cleared fields, like Plymouth, where the Pilgrims landed, open for settlement.

The original Daniel Hovey, arriving at age 17, soon moved to Agawam some 30 miles northeast of Boston. John Winthrop, the Royal Governor of the Colony, feared the French, who had settled further northeast on the New England coast, would soon encroach on Boston. He knew the French Huguenots had been trying to colonize North America since the ill-fated settlement of Fort Caroline in Florida in 1565.

There being no roads, he sent his son, who was called John the Younger, and 12 others in coastal vessels named shallops, to settle themselves at Agawam, a former Native American clearing. The move successfully blocked French settlement. John the Younger soon went on to become Governor of Connecticut. Those left at Agawam renamed it Ipswich after an English town of that name.

Daniel Hovey was one of the first settlers, indeed he may well have been one of the first twelve. He made a living as yeoman, a word important as a status symbol. A yeoman was not just a tenant farmer on the estate of some Lord as most farmers were in England. A yeoman was a freeman cultivating his own small estate. For a time he moved 90 miles west to Hadley near the Connecticut River, but there he claimed he had "suffered much at the depredations of the Native Americans." After moving back to Ipswich, he petitioned the Colonial Council asserting he "had expended much of his estate in the country's service." On the basis of a certificate from the Committee on Militia, he was awarded the full amount of his claim, eleven pounds.[12]

The 1668 Hovey House is shown below as drawn by Everett S. Hubbard in 1882.

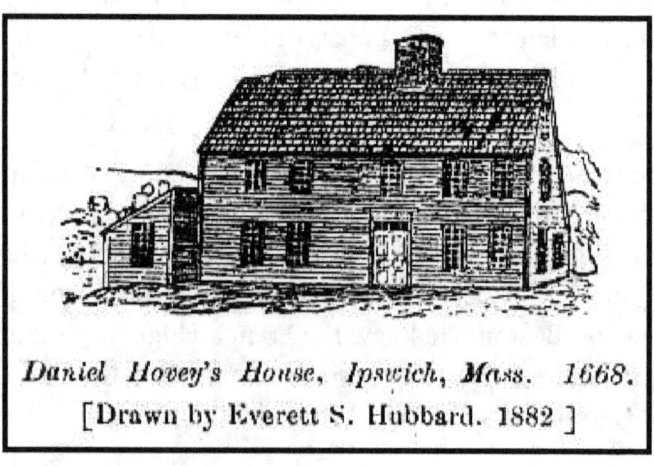

Daniel Hovey's House, Ipswich, Mass. 1668.
[Drawn by Everett S. Hubbard. 1882]

For the first half century after their arrival, these early settlers made an uneasy peace with Massasoit, the Chief of the neighboring Wampanoag tribe. After a very difficult first winter, the survivors learned how to grow corn from some Native Americans that had been captured by English traders. This supplemented the supply of seafood, fowl and game. The forests furnished ample wood for building houses.

The combination of shelter and diet—and possibly the long winter nights—led to large families. The English settlers soon outgrew the uninhabited areas, particularly the farmland that accounts for only about 20 percent of rocky New England soil. Furthermore, the introduction of flintlock muskets, which Native Americans found of great advantage in killing game and increasing the number of furs to trade, eventually led to a shortage of fur bearing animals in the wild.

Thus by 1675, faced with a shortage of fur to trade and encroachment on their land and culture, the son of Massasoit, Metacom, known to the English as King Philip, decided to make war on the English. The clash of cultures was particularly galling to the Native Americans. Some Englishmen tried to convert them to Christianity. To do so, they taught some to speak and a few to read and write the English language. Harvard College went so far as to build an Indian College. One English Missionary, John Eliot, even learned the Massachusett language and published the Bible in it. As a result there were a few towns of "praying Indians" split off from the rest of the tribes.

Meanwhile King Philip rallied a number of native tribes as far west as the Connecticut River to fight the invaders. These included the Massachusett, the Narragansett, the Nipmugs, and even the Sokonnet, headed by Awashonks, a female Sachem.[13] At first the Native Americans gained the upper hand. While the English could convert well-built houses into garrisons relatively immune from bow and arrow attacks, the Indians learned how to set these garrisons on fire. King Philip's forces killed more than 800 English settlers and in some cases cut off their fingers and toes to wear as necklaces. They also burned numerous villages and eviscerated herds of cattle, which they felt a special threat to their culture.[14] Most of these attacks were on hamlets far removed from the coast.

The Mohegan, however, was one of the inland tribes that had converted, in whole or in part, to Christianity. The Mohegans were long time enemies of the Wampanoags. These "Praying

Indians" led to King Philip's undoing. With their help, the English counterattacked with equal savagery. They virtually wiped out the Massachsett and Naragansett and in 1676 killed King Philip, set his severed head on a victory pole, and brought two years of war to an end. Many of the praying Indians were quarantined on Deer Island in the Boston Harbor and later sold as slaves.

Near the coast, the Ipswich militia thwarted Indian attacks. Thus the Hovey and other Ipswich families were saved from most of the depredations. Over the next three generations they increased their numbers exponentially. This made the available farmland much more expensive and many took to the sea or other trades. Some of the Hoveys moved to Boxford, ten miles west of Ipswich. There the third Daniel Hovey was born in 1701. Instead of farming like his father, he became an apprentice in the ancient trade of coopering.

Until the second century B.C., the fragile clay pot was the principal means of storage for shipment or transport. But in that century it was replaced by the wooden cask. The cask led to many kinds of containers, each for a specific purpose (i.e. the firkin, kilderkin, hogshead, butt, runlet, tierce, puncheon, and pipe.) The most universal container was the barrel, made with staves, bound together by hoops, and closed with flat ends. For wine and rum barrels, there is tight coopering, requiring fitted grooves and laps as in the hull of ships. For flour, corn, gunpowder and tobacco barrels, there is slack coopering. To use the drawknives and other tools of coopering, requires skill, intelligence and strength and sometimes leads to injury.

This trade enabled the third Daniel to buy a 1.25-acre lot in Branford, for 195 pounds in 1741 when he was 40 years old. It was located 12 miles to the northwest of Boxford on the Merrimack River (Algonquian for place of strong current). On this current, great logs floated downstream from New Hampshire, oak for tight coopering and pine for slack coopering. The Merrimack River also provided a seaport, Newburyport, for exporting the output of the cooperage.

In the same year he moved to Branford, which is now part of Haverhill, Massachusetts, Daniel Hovey III married Ruth, the daughter of Captain John and Anne (Messenger) Tyler of Boxford. His cooperage business as well as his family expanded in Branford over the next four years. Daniel IV was born in 1742, Anna in 1744 and Joshua in 1746. In 1747, the successful cooper, now age 46, sold his estate for 300 pounds, making a profit of more than 100 pounds. Apparently ill health or a serious injury forced him to give up his successful cooperage and retire to a farm.

He moved 70 miles southwest to Sutton, Massachusetts, where he had relatives. It was the former home of the Nipmug tribe. This tribe had been displaced in 1686 by French Huguenots. The Huguenots were Protestants who had been given certain rights in Catholic France by the Edict of Nantes. They were driven from France by King Louis XIV, who in 1685 revoked the Edict. The Huguenot Priests managed to convert some of the Nipmugs[15] to Christianity, and for a decade the Huguenots lived in peace with the "praying" Indians. When this peace broke down in 1696 the Huguenots moved to Rhode Island.

Sutton is in the beautiful valley of the Blackstone River. This river rises near Worcester and runs southeast, coursing among giant boulders sculpted in the last ice age by the sudden runoff from a glacier (purgatory Chasm). The river empties into Narragansett Bay at Pawtucket. To the west, Sutton borders Oxford, Massachusetts, in the neighboring French River Valley. The French River rises west of Worcester and eventually joins the Connecticut River.

The land between the French River west of Oxford and the Blackstone River to its east is broken by a series of small rocky hills, more suited to hardwood forests than farming. The oft-told story of how God created North America applies here. In the West he piled up the earth to make Rocky Mountains but he saw they were too high. In the center he smoothed the earth to make Great Plains but he saw they were too flat. In New England he spread his fingers apart and gently drew them across the earth to make hills and rills, and he saw they were just right.

The English acquired this land, described as a tract of wasteland twelve miles square, from John Wampus and other now peaceful Nipmugs by deed in February 1731, as approved by Joseph Dudley, the Royal Governor of the Province of Massachusetts. Gradually the English settlers cleared enough stones from the top of the hills (stones being much easier to roll down hill than up hill) to do some farming.

After several temporary stays, Daniel Hovey was fortunate enough to acquire a fifty-acre farm in Sutton, with house and barn for 106 pounds, 13 shillings and four pence. It was located on one of the very rare, relatively flat areas of Sutton. This land was just west of Oxford and was annexed by Oxford in 1793.[16] It was adjacent to a farm in Sutton owned by John Haven, a Deacon of the Sutton Anglican Church, which Daniel and his family attended.

Following the move to the Oxford area, four more children were born to Daniel and Ruth. They were Moses, born in 1748, Thomas in 1750, John Tyler in 1753 and Mary in 1755. Two of the boys Thomas and John Tyler died, as did the older Joshua. We have no written record of their deaths or the cause. The birthing of babies in those days was strictly women's work. Neighboring women gathered at the home of the child bearer, who was obliged to feed them bountifully until labor started.

There as Godmothers (they were originally called God-sibbs, and thus in addition to children, the word "gossip" was born) they acted as midwives. Having only five out of eight children survive in those days was not abnormal. Along with a high rate of infant mortality, and the usual childhood diseases, whooping cough, mumps and measles, there were epidemics of yellow fever and deadly smallpox.

George III, born June 4, 1738, was King of England from October 25, 1760–January 29, 1820. Portrait of his coronation on Sept. 22, 1761 by Allan Ramsay, 1762

CHAPTER THREE

The Tories and the Whigs

The Churches and the Taverns

The last child of Daniel and Ruth, their eighth, survived. He was Benjamin Hovey. He was born on March 12, 1758, at the 50 acre farm Daniel had bought three years earlier. This was during the time of the French and Indian War. This war had started on May 28, 1754, when 22-year-old Lieutenant Colonel George Washington, on an expedition to secure the Ohio Valley for Virginia, ordered his militia to fire on a French and Indian scouting force. This fray escalated into a war over control of the Ohio River Valley, Canada and most of North America. In Europe, where it was called the Seven Years War, the English defeated both France and Spain. The English finally prevailed both in Europe and North America. France ceded all the land east of the Mississippi claimed by it, except New Orleans, to the English by the Treaty of Paris on February 10, 1763. This war led, as most wars do, to a dispute as to who should pay for it. England had provided most of the troops, but the colonies suffered as well. The Hovey farm should have provided a fairly prosperous living for the family but wartime taxes were raised to a very high level.

Benjamin was born during the reign of King George II of England. At the time of his birth, men and women were not considered to be created equal. They owed allegiance to the hereditary King of England and to the hierarchy of the Anglican Church. In England, where most of the land was owned by hereditary noblemen, they were also beholden to their landlord who was also their Lord. Only about one-fifth of the population owned their own land. The rest relied on patronage of the Lord to whom they paid rent. He in turn relied on patronage of the King. In the American colonies where about two-thirds of the settlers owned their own land, these hereditary and patronage ties were greatly attenuated. Allegiances were more provincial. Fear of the county sheriff and the father of the family were more immediate than fear of the King, Lord or Provincial Governor.

When Benjamin was three, George III, became King of England upon the death of his grandfather, George II. The British Government had been controlled for some years chiefly by a series of strong Whig Prime Ministers, most notably William Pitt, the Elder, who attempted to reconcile with the restless American colonies. However, young George III increased his control over Britain's Constitutional Monarchy, especially after a Tory Prime Minister, Frederick Lord North, was appointed in 1770.

England had succeeding in defeating French and Spanish forces in Europe and the French and Indians in North America, but these victories had come at great financial cost. King George III insisted the colonies help pay England's debts. In 1767, the English passed the Townshend Revenue Act, imposing a tax on glass, oil, paper, lead and tea. To resist this tax, merchants throughout the colonies agreed not to import these articles, and by the time Benjamin was 12 these duties were repealed except on tea. Worcester's American Political Society, which included representatives from Oxford, was particularly concerned with the tax on tea and the effect of a change in the payment of salaries to local officials. Formerly they had been paid by the local government to which they were beholden; now they were paid by and beholden to the Crown. The Society declared that anyone selling contraband tea would be considered an enemy and if Judges accepted any money from the Crown, they were no longer bound to submit to their Orders.

The Crown had previously quartered troops in the homes of residents of Boston, a continual irritation and expense. The residents and rowdy youths so taunted the "Lobster Backs" that they fired on the crowd killing five men, the so called Boston Massacre of 1770. Committees of Correspondence were formed in many towns throughout the colonies. In the fall of 1772, the "Boston Pamphlet" was published asserting the rights of colonists. It was distributed in Oxford as well as the nearby shire town of Worcester, a hotbed of resistance to British rule. The Bostonians refused to pay the tax on tea and demanded the ships bearing it be returned to England. Governor Thomas Hutchinson refused this demand. After Bostonians met with Samuel Adams, a good many dressed as Mohawk Indians boarded three British ships, the Dartmouth, Eleanor and Beaver, on December 16, 1773, and threw 342 chests of tea overboard into Boston Harbor.

At the urging of George III for retribution, Lord North persuaded Parliament to pass a number of coercive measures in 1774. The port of Boston was closed until the East India Company was reimbursed for the cost of the tea thrown into the harbor. The Royal Governor took control of the Massachusetts government and appointed all officials, including the sheriffs. The Crown asserted the right to quarter soldiers in private homes throughout the colonies.

Benjamin learned of these events during his teenage years. There were more than 40 taverns in nearby Worcester and several in Sutton and Oxford, rallying places for the Whigs opposed to the Acts of Parliament which they deemed intolerable. In general, the Tories in both England and America were tied to and met in the Anglican Churches, while the Whigs, at least in America, more often met in homes or taverns. Thus, as Benjamin grew up, he would hear discussion of the growing dissatisfaction between the people of Massachusetts and the English governors of the colony. In particular, a pamphlet was printed in Boston to which the radicals in Worcester replied. Foreshadowing the Declaration of Independence, Thomas Bigelow, a blacksmith, and his committee declared to the Bostonians:

"It is our opinion that mankind are by nature free, and that the end and designe of forming social compacts, and entering into civil society, was that each member of that Society, might enjoy his liberty and property, and live in the free exercise of his rights, both civil and religious, which God and nature gave; except such as are expressly given up by compact."[17]

In June 1774, the Worcester radicals received the news that Parliament had revoked key provisions of the Constitution of Massachusetts. They armed themselves and forced the Tories supporting the Crown to resign. In September all Court officials were forced to march, while recanting their respective offices, through a cordon of citizens from Worcester and surrounding towns. Thus Worcester declared its Independence. It was no longer governed by George III. By October all of Massachusetts, except Boston, where British troops were stationed, was ruled by the body of the people, not the King of England. Expecting a response by British soldiers at an unknown time or place, minutemen squads were organized in each town. Benjamin was 16 so was eligible and became a minuteman.

During these turbulent times, his father, Daniel, at age 71 and in declining health, could no longer cope with both the tax burden on farmers and the decrease in demand for farm products as a result of the closing of the ports for export. He and his wife, Ruth, conveyed the farm to their son, Moses, then 23. The deed recited that the transfer was in consideration of two hundred thirty pounds. Concurrently, Moses, in consideration of the same amount, agreed to let them live in the farm homestead in rooms of their choosing, and to provide them with a most detailed list of consumables, as long as they lived. In the ancient handwritten indenture, only half of the items to be supplied yearly are legible. They are:

14 bushels of merchantable Indian corn,
One bushel of wheat,
One bushel of malt,
Four barrels of cider,
One hundred weight of good beef,
Two hundred weight of pork,
One bushel and one-half of salt,
Eight bushels of winter apples,
A quarter of a hundred of sugar,
Sufficient firewood, ready cut and delivered at the door and
On death, a good Christian burial.

This document was duly recorded on September 16, 1772. Today it would be considered most unusual, but in colonial times such lists were common, starting with lists of the items settlers should bring with them to live in New England. This list does give us a vision of the farm. We glimpse a picture of an apple orchard, a pasture for grazing beef cattle, a pen for pigs, a field for raising corn to feed both family and livestock and some patches of forest for firewood.

In addition to providing a home and food for his parents, Moses promised to pay their other living children money. Daniel, Jr. was to receive 13 pounds, 5 shillings and 8 pence one year after his father's death; Anna was to get 6 pounds, 13 shillings and 5 pence, two years thereafter, Mary 6 pounds, 13 shillings and 4 pence, three years thereafter; and finally Benjamin was to be awarded 20 pounds four years thereafter.

It seems his parents chose Moses, their fourth child, as the oldest available male to provide for them in their infirmity. Their first born, Daniel, Jr. was off courting Elizabeth Green in Malden, north of Boston and the three other sons were dead. Naturally, with the five remaining children there must have developed sibling rivalry. As the eighth and youngest child, Benjamin had to contend for attention with, at first, five older brothers and two older sisters.

One can imagine Father Daniel calling the remaining children together and reading the covenant by Moses. The parents, although rapidly failing in health, tried to divide their estate with rough justice. While Moses promised to house his parents and provide them with food and heat during their declining years, the unique indenture is silent on where Daniel, Jr., Anna, Mary and Benjamin should live and what help they were to provide about the farm.

While the farm was in Sutton, there was no free public school within walking distance. There was a free public school in nearby Oxford within walking distance, but Benjamin never attended. The only logical reasons for the omission of his primary school education are either that attendance was restricted to only residents of the same town in which the school was located — or that the Hovey household was quarantined for fear of an infectious disease; most probably smallpox. It may have carried off Joshua, Thomas and John Tyler during Benjamin's early years.

After the reading of the Indenture, it is likely the independent and restless Benjamin spent the next three years working on the farm and nearby farms such as that of Deacon John Haven, when requested, as well as working on the town roads and running errands for the Sheriff of Worcester. The Sheriff's Office had been held for some years by members of the Chandler family, who during the 1774 gauntlet running had made a seamless transition from Tory to Whig. As will be illustrated later, Benjamin was a careful and studious observer of running a farm, a sheriff's duties and especially road building.

Much of social life centered on the church in those days. There was time for gossip and exchange of views before and after the church service. Benjamin probably met Lydia Haven, the comely auburn haired daughter[18] of Deacon John Haven, at church before seeing her on her home turf while lending a hand at harvest time. Being three years older, she apparently took him under her wing and became his confidante.

At the Anglican Church, the Puritans were followers of John Calvin, not given to much frivolity. They did not even celebrate Christmas. Calvinism in its original form is a strict doctrine. Its five tenets are: first, babies inherit the original sin of Adam; second all babies are on God's master list of who will and will not be saved; third Christ died for only those on the saved list; fourth, God sends a holy spirit to the saved and inculcates in them a faith in Jesus Christ; and fifth, once saved, a complex doctrine called preservation of the saints may entitle one to enter heaven. Puritans did not believe the Church had the authority to grant indulgences to evade these tenets even through good works. This rigid doctrine banned games of chance, frivolity such as dances around maypoles, and drama. Playing with cards was considered playing with the "Devil's Tickets." In the New World, as generations succeeded one another, strict Calvinism was increasingly observed in the breach. In Oxford and Sutton, there were occasional spinning bees and even more popular quilting frolics where women met to spin thread or quilt comforters and exchange gossip over tea. There was even an ungodly tavern in Sutton, where the genial tavern keeper, Bartholomew Woodbury, encouraged tavern games and songs. Some were of a political nature, such as this one mocking the taxes being imposed on the colonies, including one on the sun's light.[19]

> One single thing untaxed at home old England could not show / For money we abroad did roam and sought to tax the new / And a taxing we will go, we'll go, we'll go / And a taxing we will go.
>
> The power supreme of Parliament our purpose did assist. / And taxing laws abroad were sent, which the rebels do resist. / And a taxing we will go, we'll go, we'll go. / And a taxing we will go.
>
> Shall we not make the rascals bend to Britain's supreme power? / The sword shall we not to them tend, and leaden balls a shower? / And a taxing we will go, we'll go, we'll go. / And a taxing we will go.
>
> We'll force and fraud in one unite to bring them to our hands, / Then lay a tax on the sun's light and a king's tax on their lands. / And a taxing we will go, we'll go, we'll go. / And a taxing we will go.

Other fun times included barn raising followed by food, hard cider, and for those who wanted even higher spirits, drawing the bung out of a barrel of rum. Frolics followed a husking bee and certainly a little cider and rum were welcome after a backbreaking "stone bee," where husky neighbors joined in rolling away the black stones that abounded in the area to create a tillable field.

CHAPTER FOUR
Seventeen Seventy-Five
The Call of Paul Revere

The year 1775 was perhaps the most eventful year in the life of Benjamin Hovey. One, he turned 17; two, he sired a child before the benefit of wedlock; three, he went off to war; four, he got married; and five, he had a baby daughter. To top the year off the day after her birth; he went off to war again. The record is clear: on the night of Paul Revere's ride, April 18/19, 1775, Benjamin was not the unknown rider bound for Tewksbury, the first man to answer the call of Paul Revere. Rather, like several thousand other minutemen, when summoned, he eagerly answered the first call of Paul Revere.

British law required that Benjamin join the Crown Militia at age 16. The Crown could call out the militia, ranging in age from 16 to 60, in time of danger. Each militiaman was required to have a firelock, a bayonet and a quantity of ammunition. The Whig Committee on Safety grafted secret minutemen companies modeled on the Crown's requirements. Such a secret company existed in Sutton after the Courts were shut down by the radicals in nearby Worcester. News of Revere's call to arms reached Sutton within an hour or two after the news reached Worcester, just before noon on April 19. Thus, the Sutton Company could not have reached the bloody retreat of the Redcoats from Concord and Lexington to Bunker Hill until late on April 20.

The baby daughter, named Ruth, after Benjamin's mother, was born on December 8, 1775. Benjamin had married Lydia Haven, a 20-year-old lass, on October 24, 1775, just 45 days before the baby arrived. As mentioned, they may have met at church or as harvest help. Lydia lived on an adjacent farm just over the line in Sutton. She was the daughter of John Haven, a Deacon of the Anglican Church. As such, according to the Bible[20], holding the mystery of the faith in a pure conscience, "Let the deacons be the husband of one wife, ruling their children and their own houses well." We can only imagine how distraught the Deacon and his wife Susanna were when they learned of such an "ill-ruled" event; their unmarried daughter Lydia was pregnant.

Their mortification must have multiplied when they heard that the father was Benjamin; so young, uneducated and only occasionally employed by the Sherriff. As for Benjamin, at 17, he felt, no doubt, unready to take on the responsibility of a family. As for Lydia she must have realized she had only four choices: first, to persuade Benjamin to marry her; second, to have the baby and raise it herself; third, to have the baby and give it up for adoption; and fourth to have an abortion. In those days only the first option was acceptable. As the baby quickened on schedule in its mother's womb and as the pregnancy neared the ninth month, pressure must have been brought to bear on the couple to announce their intention to marry. The law required them to notify the town clerk of their intention at least three weeks before the wedding date. The law further required that a notice be posted at least three weeks before the wedding date to permit persons to object. It seems probable that Benjamin's mother, Ruth, was the most ready to forgive the transgression of the couple and help nurture her granddaughter, Ruth, who was

Paul Revere

A portrait by John Singleton Copley, circa 1770
(Museum of Fine Arts, Boston)

named for her. Further confirming the split with the Havens, not one of the children of Benjamin and Lydia was named for the Mother's ancestors as was customary for genteel families at the time.

Please note that December is the eighth month after April when Lydia may have conceived her child. In the small houses of early colonial days, parents often sewed their daughter in a bundling bag for a semi-chaste night of snuggles and sleep with a potential mate, but with the building of larger houses, bundling had fallen into disrepute. Thus the more romantic among us can imagine the following scenario:

* * *

A little before noon on April 19, 1775, a rider, say, Squire Learned, pulls up in front of the Hovey farmhouse. "Benjamin" he calls. A well built young man of about five feet ten inches of height with the square jaw, grey-green eyes and aquiline nose common in his descendents appears.[21] "Yes Squire," he answers "What is it?" "The British have attacked our militia in Concord and Lexington. They say the Redcoats fired first. A dozen or more are dead and many wounded. You are to report to Captain Woodbury's company by three o'clock. Don't forget your musket, ammunition and food for three days." "Meet at the tavern at three?" "Yes, I'll see you there. We march for Boston this afternoon." Benjamin dashes into the house and tells sister, Anna, the news. Anna says "I'll get your rations ready."

Then he must tell his confidante, Lydia Haven, that he is now going off to war. She used to treat him as little brother, but he has grown to be a man now, a man with a firm jaw, broad chest and rippling muscles; besides she has been friendlier lately. At church, she always sat in the second row of pews with her family and the Deacon when he was not speaking. From the Hoveys' usual pew several rows to the rear, Benjamin could just see her left ear, cheek and wavy auburn curls. Whenever the sermon got boring, as it almost always did, he would lapse in to a recurrent daydream. Brother Moses had agreed to let him ride Rex to the entrance to the trail to Purgatory Chasm and Lydia had condescended to go with him, she riding on her mare, Old Nel. When they reached the chasm's entrance, they dismounted, tethered their horses and squeezed through the narrow gate of boulders called Fat Man's Misery. From there they had scrambled down the rocky trail as far as Lovers Leap for a striking view of the dry black Purgatory Chasm etched in the granite bedrock some 70 feet below. It looked as if the Lord had taken a cleaver to make a rift in the Earth's crust, then quit and tossed in a few angular boulders as an afterthought. Then, just as Ben was about to lead Lydia to a hidden cave that only he knew, the minister would finally reach his peroration and startle Ben out of his romantic reverie.

To see her, Ben ran up the hill, vaulting, as lithely as a white-tailed deer, over the stone wall that marks the boundary between Oxford and Sutton, trotting past the barren as yet unplanted corn field to the next farmhouse. "Mrs. Haven," he called, "Where's Lydia?"

"Out in the barn, currying Old Nel."

Benjamin found Lydia leading Old Nel back to her stall. He blurted out, "Lydia, the British troops have attacked the minutemen at Concord and Lexington and killed and wounded many minutemen!"

"Oh Benjamin, have you been called up?"

"Old Nel Whinnied" by F. Charles Woodruff

"Yes, Squire Learned rode by. I have to report to Captain Kingsbury's Company at three. Sister Anna is preparing my rations. We march for Roxbury Camp near Boston, tonight."

"Oh, Benjamin, you could be killed. Goodness, this is the last time I may ever see you. Let me give you a hug and a kiss for good luck."

Except in his daydream, this had never happened. He hastily jumped at the chance. In leaping forward to her outstretched arms, he tripped over the handle of a pitchfork. They fell back together into a soft pile of hay. He felt her firm breasts against his shirt and her mouth against his.

"Benjamin, what a clumsy boy you are," she laughed, then gently brushed his hair away from her face and unbuttoned his shirt. They were both ablaze and amazed in a moment, a firmament of rainbows, shooting stars and rockets, more transcendent than anything they had ever felt before. They might have remained in the hay all afternoon but Old Nel jolted them back to reality with a loud whinny. Benjamin hastily pulled on his pants, tucked in his shirt and with a final kiss and squeeze of her hand left the blushing Lydia to report to his company.

Whether this fruitful liaison occurred as suggested in the above scenario or earlier in a surreptitious meeting on a cold winter's night, its details are known only to Benjamin and Lydia, but their passions have been shared by others since the time of Adam and Eve.

* * *

Whatever the case may be, on April 20, 1775, Colonel Artemas Ward, the Commander in Chief of the Colonial Massachusetts Militia, left a sick bed to reach his troops, or perhaps more correctly his rabble, surrounding Boston. Pursuant to his orders,

General John Thomas, commander of the Regiment at Roxbury sent out parties to bury the dead, collect food supplies and build earthworks. General Thomas commented in a letter to John Adams "The Regiments at Roxbury, the privates are equal to any I have served with in the last war,..."[22]

Thus, Benjamin's first taste of Army life was not battle, but work detail. April nights can be right chilly in Boston. And at first there were no tents. Sitting up half the night huddled by a fire, he listened to many tales of the action as the Redcoats beat their bloody way back to Bunker Hill. After two nights in the cold he may have gone to a nearby farm to ask for a blanket. On the way he may have met a fellow from Oxford of about his age on the same mission. The farmer doubtless told them, "You lads are behind about a dozen fellows who have been here before you. I have given away even the horse blanket and every scrap of sailcloth! The only things I've got to spare are some empty sacks." They gladly accepted these and tied them together to improvise a tiny tent, which they shared at night. Soon they became fast friends and joined in a taunting song composed by an Irishman named Paddy.

> By my faith, but I think you're all makers of bulls, With your brains in your breeches, your guts in your skulls. / Get home with your muskets and put up your swords, / And look on your books for the meaning of words. / You see now, my honies, how much you're mistaken, / For Concord by discord can never be beaten.
>
> How brave you went out with your muskets all bright, / And sought to befrighten the folks with the fight; / But when you got there how they powered your pums; / All the way home, how they peppered your bums. / And isn't it, honies, of comical cheer / To be proud in

the face and shot in the rear?

And what have you got now with all your designing. / But a town without victuals to sit down and dine in; / And look on the ground like a parcel of noodles / And sing, how the Yankees have beaten the doodles. / I'm sure if you're wise you'll make peace for a dinner / For fighting and fasting will soon make you thinner.

There is a small peninsula, the Charlestown Peninsula, sticking down like an overstuffed Christmas stocking from the north side of the Charles River into the bay across from the City of Boston. At the heel of the stocking is Charlestown. Above it is Breed's Hill; then toward the narrow top of the stocking is Bunker Hill. Soon the British left the Charlestown Peninsula and retreated across the bay to Boston. After only 17 days of service, marked mostly by work detail and the occasional exchange of shots between opposing sentries, the Sutton Company went home. They returned in time to plant the farm crops by the middle of May, 1775.

Late in June, news reached Sutton of another bloody battle. Generals Artemas Ward and Israel Putnam, "Old Put," head of the Connecticut Militia, found out that the British were planning to reoccupy the Charlestown Peninsula. They constructed a redoubt and fortifications on Breed's Hill above Charlestown. The British, whose Navy commanded the bay, landed troops under the command of General Howe on the eastern tip or toe of the stocking and commenced a frontal assault on Breed's Hill. Despite fierce defense by Continental troops, they retook Breed's Hill at great cost and then up the peninsula retook Bunker Hill, again at great cost. It had been ably and stubbornly defended by troops under Colonel John Stark, later famous for the defense of the supplies stored at Bennington, Vermont.

In winning the battle of Bunker Hill, the British lost 1,500 killed and wounded, including 138 officers, as opposed to only 450 casualties of the militia under Generals Ward and Putnam. After taking such serious losses, the British fortified the Charlestown Peninsula and hunkered down in Boston under a state of siege. Although they were the victors, one of their Generals, Sir Henry Clinton, remarked, "A few more such victories would surely put an end to British dominion in America." The stout fight of these troops encouraged General George Washington to set off for Boston.

On July 1, 1775, the news reached Sutton that General Washington was on his way to take command of the Continental Army. He had just ridden to Mary Stearn's Tavern in nearby Worcester. The next day, resplendent in the eye-catching blue uniform of the Virginia Militia, he rode into camp near Boston tall in the saddle on a great white horse.[23] He replaced the ailing General Ward and also General Putnam as head of the up to 14,000 troops spread over a nine-mile circle pinning the British in Boston.

He immediately introduced military drill, and took other measures to bring discipline. In addition to discipline, Washington had to provide food, improve sanitation and construct better quarters. Without shelter his predecessors had raided all the seaport towns for discarded sails to be used as makeshift tents for the mixture of militia and enlisted Continental soldiers that made up the forces confining the British soldiers in Boston. He soon found in these troops a mixed multitude, both a high-spirited punch and a stew.

The high-spirited punch consisted of two ingredients, a sprinkling of genuine patriots, such as Daniel Shays and Josiah Hackett (of whom more later) and also sturdy yeoman who signed on to fight, but only until their enlistments expired, or in

Washington rode a white charger into Boston, not his favorite horse, a chestnut hunter.

some cases even if unexpired, it was time to plant the crops. Of these, Washington said: "The deficiency in their numbers, their discipline and stores, can only lead to this conclusion, that their spirit has exceeded their strength."[24] The stew, indeed a veritable slumgullion, consisted of unreliable n'er do wells, outcasts, drop-outs and loners, some of whom never before had it so good.

The Connecticut Militia under General Israel Putnam understood their enlistments ended December 1 and attempted to depart then. However the actual date was December 10. Under threat of imprisonment or other disciplinary action, most stayed until the tenth. To remedy the loss of the Connecticut troops, General Washington called up 5,000 militiamen from Massachusetts and New Hampshire. Among these was the Sutton militia. Benjamin Hovey marched for Boston on December 9, 1775, just the day after Lydia, his bride of six weeks, gave birth to their daughter, Ruth.

Benjamin was in the Company of Sutton's genial tavern keeper, Captain Bartholomew Woodbury. On December 11, Washington reported to Congress that the militia are coming fast. "I am much pleased with the alacrity, which the good people of the province, as well as those of New Hampshire, have shown on this occasion. I expect the whole will be in this day or tomorrow when the Connecticut gentry who have not enlisted will have liberty to go to their firesides."[25] With the arrival of the militia, concern for the loss of the Connecticut troops soon passed. Morale improved when barracks went up, firewood was brought in and Mrs. Washington arrived in Cambridge to spend the winter with her husband.

The stand off between Washington's army in training surrounding Boston and Howe's battle-tested regulars in the city had lasted all summer and into the fall until a young Colonel, Henry Knox, completed a remarkable feat of transportation.

Knox and his men hauled the large cannons installed to defend Fort Ticonderoga at the foot of New York's Adirondack Mountains all the way to Boston. Despite the winter weather, they came first by boat down Lake George, then by caisson or where snow was sufficient by long sleds, hauled by oxen to the west bank of the Hudson River. They successfully crossed the frozen river at Albany, except for one large cannon that broke through the ice near the eastern shore. It was with great effort recovered, and hauled over the Berkshire Mountains, across the frozen Connecticut River. Then switching to the less ponderous and quicker power of horses, the sleds were hauled all the way to Dorchester Heights overlooking the City of Boston from the southwest.

As the cannons approached Boston, Benjamin and his Company were hard at work fortifying the heights. The frost ran so deep in the ground that Colonel Rufus Putnam suggested that earthworks be built on top of the frozen hardscrabble atop Dorchester Heights. There was plenty of brushwood available to bundle into fascines, held in wooden frames called chandeliers. Looking more formidable than they were in actuality, the troops erected them quickly and filled them with hay hauled to the top of the heights. Hovey and scores of other young yeoman soldiers, who were far better acquainted with erecting barns and houses than with military drill, worked diligently. In addition to these gun emplacements the soldiers filled rows of barrels with rocks and placed them around the works. They not only fortified them, but also the barrels could be rolled down the hill in case of a frontal assault. This all happened so quickly, practically overnight, that a deserter reported that General Howe exclaimed: "Good God! Those fellows have done more work in one night than I can make my army do in three months. What shall I do?"[26] The cannons protruding from the fascines and other fortifications on the heights put the Redcoats in a precarious position.

Howe responded by shelling the heights with minimal effect. As Yankee privateers made provisioning Boston increasingly difficult, General Howe agreed to refrain from burning Boston to the ground if allowed to abandon his positions in peace. The last of the British and numerous civilian Tories, still loyal to King George III, left Boston on March 17, 1776, in a fleet of ships bound for Halifax, Nova Scotia. This served as a safe base to prepare an expedition for landing in New York so as to split New England from Pennsylvania, Virginia and the other southern colonies.

CHAPTER FIVE

The Founding of Universalism

All Men are created Equal; it is by "the Lord's mercies that we are not consumed."[27]

With the British gone from Boston, Benjamin was torn between two choices. He could accept the seemingly generous bonus in Continental dollars being offered to militiamen who would sign on for a three-year hitch in the Continental Army, or he could return home to his wife and child. He was particularly torn because some of his new friends had decided to enlist in the Continental Army. Benjamin had already missed his first Christmas with his family. No doubt, at the time they were being urged by their families to marry, Lydia had coyly asked, "Benjamin, do you not love me?" Likely Benjamin paused, not yet having reflected on the nature of love, let alone whether he was in love or not, but then his vision of being with Lydia in that Purgatory Chasm cave known only to him came to mind and he responded, "Oh, yes, I do!" He did like her comely looks, her lovely skin and mischievous smile. And he was proud to be a father and wanted to cradle little Ruth in his arms.

So putting first things first, he did return to Lydia and Ruth, but his attention must have been frequently interrupted by the tide of independence sweeping through the colonies—

independence from two hierarchies, the King and the Church. Thomas Paine's pamphlet *Common Sense* became widely available and, with help reading, Benjamin was exposed to new ideas. The pamphlet mocked the hereditary right of Kings by such biting comments as "One of the strongest natural proofs of the folly of hereditary Kings is that nature disapproves, otherwise she would not so readily turn it into ridicule, by giving mankind an ass for a lion." Inspired by this and similar ideas, the militia returned home believing that government should henceforth be based on the consent of the governed and Churches should be supported by the consent of the parishioners.

Shortly after his return he may have received his bequest of twenty pounds. He bought a house from George W. Gibson. He sold it and later bought the home of Dr. Learned in North Oxford which he sold in 1785. At that time the existing law compelled land holders to pay a tax to support the old, established Church. Benjamin, and other Oxford residents who had returned from service in the Revolutionary War, including a distant cousin, Hovey Davis, preferred to make "free contributions" from time to time to support such Universalist ministers as Reverend Adam Streeter. Reverend Streeter and his successors preached the doctrine of the Universalist treatise, *What Love Jesus Christ Has for Sinners*. The idea of universal redemption had been around in various forms since the time of Plato. It appears in the Bible in some form in both the Old Testament (see Lamentations 3:22) and the New Testament (see Mark, 3:28-29) and was espoused by Origen of Alexandria, who died for his views in the Third Century, A.D.[28] This idea was in sharp contrast to the Calvinists, who relied heavily on the stick of Hell rather than the carrot of Heaven.

The Universalist tradition of there being one God, who believed in love, universally pardoning all sinners, was carried on by Hosea Ballou. He was ordained in Oxford, Massachusetts, by what is said to be the earliest Universalist Society established in America. Universalist beliefs and congregations spread both northward to Canada and southward to Philadelphia and ultimately as far as Georgia. They were articulated by the Winchester Profession of 1803, recognizing that both the Holy Scriptures of the Old and New Testaments and other religions contain revelations. At one time, Universalists constituted the ninth largest denomination in the country.

Benjamin and Lydia signed the original compact establishing this first Universalist Society in 1785. Unlike early Unitarians, who often were wealthy, Harvard educated, and upper class, Universalists were generally small land-holders and less educated, as were the Hoveys.[29] Over the years the class distinctions between Unitarians and Universalists disappeared and these two non-Trinitarian denominations merged in 1961.

Back in 1785, membership in this society not only relieved the Hoveys from allegiance to a church whose beliefs condemned them to Hell, as well as their child who had been born so soon after wedlock, but also from being taxed to support such a church. That was surely independence in action!

Such independence had taken many years to secure. On July 2, 1776, the Declaration of Independence was approved by the Continental Congress and inscribed on parchment. It was first signed two days later on July Fourth. Its approval inspired John Adams to say: "The second day of July 1776 will be the most venerable epocha (sic) in the history of America. I am apt to believe that it will be celebrated by succeeding generations as the great anniversary festival. It ought to be commemorated as the Day of Deliverance, by solemn acts of devotion to God Almighty. It ought to be solemnized with pomp and parade, with shows, games, sports, bells, bonfires and illuminations, from one end of this continent to the other, from this time forward forever more."[30] Except for the date being two days early, how prescient he was!

Printed copies of the Declaration of Independency, as it was then called, reached Worcester in the latter part of July 1776. A great crowd assembled on July 22 near the Liberty Pole and bells were set a ringing and drums a beating. This was followed by hurrahs, the firing of musketry and cannon. Some twenty-five toasts, washed down with rum and wine, were made, starting with:

> "*Prosperity and perpetuity to the United States of America*" ... and ending with:
>
> "*May the freedom and independency of America endure 'til the sun grows dim with age, and the earth returns to chaos.*"[31]

News of this great document and the celebration reached Oxford quickly. From Benjamin's point of view, the most profound, revolutionary and uplifting idea was the self-evident truth that "all men are created equal." A cooper, like his father, or a yeoman like himself, was born equal to the wealthiest merchant in Boston or the richest planter in the south or the King of England for that matter. But he also realized that all men did not stay equal; some were highly educated, and others like himself had received no formal education.

Adding to the great news that Independence had been declared, was word from South Carolina that the British fleet and British General Sir Henry Clinton had been repulsed at Sullivan's Island by Continental General Charles Lee on June 29, 1776, leaving Charleston, South Carolina, in Continental hands.

Meanwhile, indeed on the day before July 4, a royal fleet of 130 ships assembled in New York Harbor. It was commanded by Vice Admiral Richard Howe, the older brother of Major General William Howe. Their elder brother, George, had been killed near Ticonderoga in 1758 during the French and Indian War. In Parliament Richard had voted against the Coercive Acts that bred the revolt. Both the Admiral and General felt attached to the colonies. They attempted to negotiate a peace while the British troops landed and bivouacked on Staten Island, but had no authority to recognize the independence of the colonies. After all peace negotiations failed, military engagements commenced when the British troops landed on Long Island on August 21, 1776. They defeated the Continental troops led by George Washington in Brooklyn, then ousted them from Manhattan. Benjamin may have heard personal accounts of the battle in Brooklyn from his friends given a furlough. Some had spent all summer working on the fortifications on Brooklyn Heights and had fired a 12 pounder cannon at distant British troops, but were then ordered to spike the cannons and retreat to Manhattan Island on a foggy night

Indeed, the British controlled New York City for seven years until the Treaty of Paris ended the War in 1783. Of more immediate concern to Benjamin Hovey, the Howe brothers decided to better bottle up the Revolutionary shipping by controlling Rhode Island's ocean access.

The British fleet sailed into Narragansett Bay early in December, 1776. On December 7 they landed 6,000 British troops commanded by Major General Richard Prescott at Newport. Newport is near the southern end of Aquidneck Island in the bay. Fearing an invasion of the rest of Rhode Island, the Massachusetts Militia was again called out and with it Benjamin Hovey, for his third service during the Revolutionary War. He was a Private in Colonel Jonathan Holman's Sutton Regiment. He served 43 days in the Company of Captain Jeremiah Kingsbury. The Company marched about 40 miles from Sutton to Pawtucket and Providence, at the head of the bay to protect the coastal areas from further attack.[32] While on this assignment, the company heard that Washington, who had been defeated in every engagement since the British landed on Long Island, finally had a victory. He succeeded in crossing the Delaware and routing the Hessians in Trenton, New Jersey, on Christmas Eve. A few days later more good news, Washington had defeated British forces at Princeton.

Since the British at Newport had succeeded in their principal objective, blocking colonial shipping from using Narragansett Bay, they attempted no other excursions into Rhode Island. With spring planting in the offing, most of the militia withdrew to their farms. The British garrison was left at ease except for the following story well told in a Boston Newspaper: "Thursday evening last [July 10, 1777] a party of thirty-eight men [plus seven volunteers] under the command of Lieutenant Colonel William Barton ... went in five boats to Warwick Neck, with a view to take Major General Prescott ... whose headquarters were in a house about four miles from Newport. The Colonel and his party ... about twelve at night ... got to Prescott's quarters undiscovered. A sentinel at the door hailed, but was immediately secured, and the party instantly breaking the doors and entered the house took the General in his bed. His aide-de-camp leaped from a window in his shirt and attempted to escape, but was taken a few rods from the house. The party soon returned to their boats with their prisoners."[33] Even the *London Chronicle* picked up on the truly naked truth:

> "On General Prescott being carried off naked,
> unannointed, unannealed, What various lures

there are to ruin man, Woman the first and foremost, all bewitches, A nymph thus spoil'd a General's mighty plan, And gave him to the foe-without his breeches."

We do not know whether Benjamin was one of the volunteers, but we know he would have loved to have been one. We do know this was a most important capture. Washington now had a General of equal rank to exchange for General Charles Lee, one of his most trusted subordinates. Lee, early one morning, had been captured by the British at a New Jersey Inn also without his breeches, but at least he was in a dressing gown and was sitting at a table where he was writing letters, presumably on military rather than personal affairs.

A year after the capture of Major General Prescott in August 1777, General John Sullivan attempted to oust the British Garrison from Nantucket. This plan was made by General Washington and Admiral Charles-Henry-Theodat D'Estaing, commander of a French fleet that arrived on the American Coast in July 1778. D'Estaing spoke no English, but the Marquis de Lafayette, a brilliant young French officer, who Washington treated as almost the son[34] he never could have, served as translator. The glory seeking Lafayette wanted to retake the city of New York, but D'Estaing learned his twelve ships of the line had too deep a draft to enter New York Harbor. Instead, Washington and D'Estaing agreed on a plan to recapture Newport. The plan was for Sullivan to call up as many militia as he could and Lafayette to come join him with two thousand Continental troops. They would coordinate with D'Estaing, who would land a body of French troops from the sea. Lafayette would head the combined American-French force. This arrangement did not suit Sullivan in the least; he wanted to attack first. This controversy was blown away like and by the wind, when the British fleet showed up to challenge the French and both were battered and scattered by a violent storm. In fact, D'Estaing's flagship lost both its mast and its rudder. With some of his seaworthy ships, Admiral D'Estaing helped Sullivan extract the troops Sullivan had prematurely landed on the island and his fleet limped into Boston for several months of repairs.

Accordingly, Benjamin never received a fourth call to serve with the Massachusetts militia. His three relatively brief stints as a soldier in the Revolutionary War were not uncommon. Many of its battles included state militia hastily called up to defend local objectives and soon disbanded. After his defeat at Bennington by forces commanded by now General John Stark in the fall of 1777, General John Burgoyne accurately summarized this situation.[35]

> "The great bulk of the country is with the Congress in principle and zeal; and their measures are executed with a secrecy and dispatch that are not to be equaled. Wherever the King's forces point, militia to the amount of three or four thousand assemble in twenty-four hours; they bring with them their subsistence, etc., and the alarm over, they return to their farms. ..."

Only 18 years old with a family to support, Benjamin had been recommended to Gardner Chandler, Sheriff of Worcester County, as a lad who knew the area and could help serve process and perform other duties in this large County. Benjamin could no longer count on borrowing Rex, who was steady at plowing but not quick at trotting. He may have borrowed or made enough to purchase a wonderful riding horse, a roan Narragansett Pacer.[36] This breed, descended from Libyan ancestors, had recently been established in Rhode Island. A steed that paced instead of trotting made the long rides often required to carry out his duties less tiring. As a witness of that, he may have named the horse Quick Writ.

Hovey could support his horse with sporadic income from the sheriff, but not his growing family. Alphena was born on June 22, 1778.[37] Accordingly Benjamin bought a larger farm, but the land was poor and he put duties for the sheriff ahead of farm work. The population in New England had increased to a point that made it impossible to purchase good farm land except at an exorbitant price, but events in 1778 and 1779 would ultimately make much land in New York available.

George Clinton, General, Seven times Governor of New York & two times Vice President of the United States

CHAPTER SIX
Governor Clinton
Defeat of the Iroquois

George Clinton was born in 1739 on a farm in New Britain, a hamlet west of the Hudson in New York. His Presbyterian parents had immigrated from Catholic Ireland. At that time the Algonquin Indian tribes of Long Island and the Hudson River had been scattered by the Dutch and English immigrants, but much of the state west of Albany was occupied by the Iroquois Nation.

Some 200 years before Clinton was born, an Iroquois peacemaker proposed the union of all Iroquois tribes and his proposal was eloquently advocated and eventually carried out by Hiawatha. He persuaded five tribes, the Cayuga, Mohawk, Oneida, Onondaga and Seneca, to form the Iroquois Nation. Each tribe was represented by one or more elected or appointed sachems and took united action in Council with the <u>concurrence of all five tribes</u>. Later the Tuscarora became the sixth tribe to join this Nation and its sachems were included in the Council but could not vote. This was not a nation of mere hunters and gatherers. It was a proud nation of corn cultivators with fields, houses and villages living west of the Hudson River throughout the Finger Lake Region of New York State and adjacent areas.

The Colonial Governors had attempted to clothe expansion west with some scintilla of legality. For example, on April 19, 1708, a cousin of the English Queen Anne, Edward Hyde, Viscount Cornbury, the lame duck Governor of the Colony of New York, granted Johannes Hardenburgh and his associates, a patent covering up to two million acres to the west of Kingston, New York. This came about because the gentry of Kingston, New York, had applied for a patent on some farmland outside Kingston. Major Hardenburgh, miffed because he was not asked to join this select group, made an appeal in person to Lord Cornbury, who cross-dressed every Thursday as his cousin, Queen Anne. The patentees' fragile claim to this land was first, that they had purchased it from Chief Nisinos, Sachem of the Esopus Tribe for 60 pounds, and second, that it was vacant. In fact, it was not vacant for two other Indian Chiefs, Wintoon and Cahoonzie[38] had hunted in those lands now called the Catskill Mountains and did not recognize Nisinos as its owner. Nevertheless, dressed as Queen Anne, Lord Cornbury granted Hardenburgh and his associates a Royal Patent to this vast domain.

Also in 1708, Queen Anne, a devout Protestant, took pity on some 3,000 Palatine Germans who were being persecuted in their homeland for holding that faith. She assisted their immigration to England, but the English found it quite a burden to feed and clothe the new arrivals. Queen Anne solved this problem by transshipping them to the Colonies in America. Here again they were shifted about by the Colonial Governors until they landed in the lap of Robert Hunter, who had succeeded Lord Cornbury as Governor of New York.

Governor Hunter was no dim wit; he quickly solved the problem. The Iroquois tribes in the Mohawk Valley were constantly harassing and scalping the early English and Dutch settlers. Why not use the Germans as a buffer? So Hunter settled the Germans to the west of the earlier settlers and there they thrived. They lessened the conflict with the Iroquois. This permitted them to make this land the premier hop-growing area in the Colonies and to brew beer.

It was during this uneasy peace that Clinton grew up. He assisted his father who made his living by the sale of produce from the family farm and by surveying. The peace lasted until Clinton reached age 18 when the French and Indian War commenced. He joined the British Army and rose to Lieutenant by that War's end. Next he studied and practiced law, which led to frequent trips to Kingston, New York, the seat of Ulster County. There he met and married Cornelia Tappan, a relative of one of New York's landed "patroon" families. This entré to the elite, few in number, combined with his down to earth start as a yeoman farmer and surveyor, led to a successful political career.

He was selected by a popularly elected Provincial Congress to be one of its three representatives to the Second Continental Congress in Philadelphia. There he met Washington and they found that they had much in common. They both were farmers and surveyors. They both had served in the French and Indian War. They both fervently believed in the cause of Independence and both were interested in profit from land transactions. During the desperate winters of 1776 and 1777, Clinton and New York State frequently responded to Washington's appeals for food. Washington appointed Clinton, who was already a Brigadier General of State Militia, as also a Brigadier General in the Continental Army. In 1777 Clinton was elected Governor under New York's first Constitution, but his primary job was military, keeping the British forces in New York City from sailing up the Hudson River and marching up its banks to Albany.

The British had a three-fold plan to divide the Colonies. General Burgoyne from Canada to the North led the largest force, more than 5,000 men, headed south to Albany via Lake Champlain. General Sir Henry Clinton (a distant cousin) to the South had the second largest force, 4,000 men and forty ships headed north up the Hudson. Colonel Barrimore St. Leger from the west had the smallest force, 1,000 men, many of them Indians, headed east along the Mohawk River. These three forces were supposed to join in Albany. Although this was the plan, the authorities in Great Britain failed to issue direct orders to British Generals Howe in Philadelphia or Sir Henry Clinton in New York City to aid Burgoyne.

To repel the forces coming up the Hudson, Governor Clinton had established two small forts on the west side of the river, guarding the chain that had been placed across the river to stop the British fleet. They were Fort Clinton, on the south side of the Popolopen Kill, a creek plunging down from the Hudson Highlands, and Fort Montgomery on its north side. He commanded Fort Montgomery and his older brother, General James Clinton, Fort Clinton. The British brought more than 2,000 of their 4,000 troops across the Hudson to attack the 600 defenders in the two Forts. When asked to surrender to such an overwhelming number, Lieutenant Colonel Livingston replied the New Yorkers were prepared to fight to the last extremity, and indeed they did in an all day battle. After losing about 300 men and 15 officers, the British took the Forts at dusk. About half the New Yorkers survived and escaped to the Highlands, with Governor Clinton unscathed and his brother James badly wounded by a bayonet.

While the British went on to burn Kingston, New York's Provisional Capital, the cost of this victory together with the tardy arrival of militia from Connecticut under "Old Put" at his rear, prevented the British force under Sir Henry Clinton from joining up with General Burgoyne's forces. This was the first of four keys to General Gates' victory at Saratoga later in October 1777.

The other keys were second, General John Starks, who rallied a hastily gathered militia force with the admonition "We'll lick the Redcoats today lads, or Molly Stark will sleep a widow tonight."[39] And lick the Redcoats, the British force attempting to capture the arsenal at Bennington, they did. Third, General Herkimer gave up his life to stop the British/Iroquois and Colonel Barrimore St. Ledger in the Mohawk Valley. Fourth, Gates' elitist, aristocratic, unpopular predecessor, General Philip Schuyler, slowed Burgoyne's progress by felling trees to impede his path and burned crops and stores, even those on his own northern farm,[40] to reduce Burgoyne's provisions.

Burgoyne was defeated late in October 1777 at Saratoga, by American forces under the command of General Horatio Gates, a former British officer who had started his military career in England in the same regiment as Burgoyne. This defeat had major military and diplomatic consequences. The British decided to abandon Philadelphia. They retreated across New Jersey in the summer of 1778 and blunting the Continental's attack in the Battle of Monmouth, concentrated their northern forces in New York City. They detached forces to invade Georgia and the Carolinas. More important (some historians claim the Battle of Saratoga was the most important battle in the last thousand years)[41] the French decided to enter the war against the British.

The war in the north from 1778 until it ended in 1782 was virtually a stalemate. From 1778 until the end of the Revolution four years later, there were really two New York states. Six down state counties were controlled primarily by the British (New York, Kings, Queens, Richmond, Suffolk and most of Westchester) and — excluding two counties seeking to establish an independent Vermont — six upstate counties were primarily controlled by the newly established State of New York (Albany, Charlotte, Duchess, Orange, Ulster and Tryon).

One of the many problems faced by the wartime Governor and head of the militia was attacks by some tribes of the Iroquois Nation on the western frontier, a granary of not only New York but also Washington's Continental Army. One attack, the massacre at Chestnut Woods took place on September 5, 1778. There, only 30 miles west of Kingston, Lieutenant John Graham was killed with nineteen of his men.[42] Others took place in Cherry Valley. One family[43], informed by a friendly Indian that a raiding party was coming, hurriedly left their home to take refuge in the woods. The Grandmother in the family, although more than ninety years of age, remembered that her pewter spoons had been left in the house and hurried back to get them. When the family learned the raiders had gone on, they returned only to find Granny hanging by her thumbs in the apple tree next to the house, scalped and dead.[44] Some time later, on November 10 and 11, 1778, a force of 700 Indians and Tories committed the infamous Cherry Valley Massacre, killing many women and children, during a sleet storm.

As Governor Clinton had heeded General Washington's pleas for provisions, General Washington now heeded Clinton's pleas for protection of the frontier. Washington ordered Major General John Sullivan to protect the frontier by conducting a war of attrition against the tribes of the Iroquois Nation siding with the British. (Although the Iroquois were a vigorous and intelligent people, the sachems of the Nation could never unanimously agree on which side to back so each tribe was left on its own.) Washington ordered that the villages of enemy tribes be destroyed, their crops burned, and they and their English allies defeated in battle. The plan was to assemble a force equal to one- third of the Continental Army by joining forces from

Pennsylvania and New York at Tioga, where the Susquehanna River crosses the line between these States. The logistical problem was to get the New York forces commanded by General James Clinton defending the Mohawk Valley to Tioga, some 200 miles away, before the British and their Indian allies realized they were gone. This was accomplished by building 200 bateaux and damming Lake Otsego (of Glimmer Glass fame). Then the waters were released so as to create a rapid current to float the bateaux, each filled with eight men and equipment, a total of 1,600 New York troops, down the Susquehanna River all the way from Cooperstown to Tioga in two or three days.

The two forces were joined in August 1778. Only ten days thereafter the only major battle of the campaign took place at Newton near Elmira. In it the Indians, British and Tories were defeated. Thereafter forty Indian villages were destroyed and their cropland burned. Winter set in and without shelter and food, many Iroquois starved or retreated to Canada. Thus, only remnants of the Iroquois Nation were left to block expansion to the west.

Except for frontier raids and skirmishes, a stalemate ensued in the northern states. After General Horatio Gates and the Continental forces had defeated General John Burgoyne in the battle of Saratoga in October 1777, the British shifted their offensive operations to the south. They took Charleston and Savannah. The Continental Army under General Washington avoided major battles. It focused on holding the British in the City of New York and stopping foraging parties, but itself needed food. For example, on June 16, 1780, Sutton officials asked Moses Hovey to recruit 36 soldiers. Two months later he was asked to procure 17,250 pounds of beef for the Continental Army and in December an additional 33,640 pounds. Benjamin assisted his brother in all these endeavors, riding far and wide to find farmers willing to sell their beef cattle for Continental dollars.

Finally, after bitter fighting through the south, Lord Cornwallis was pinned at Yorktown, Virginia, between the Continental Army and French troops at his front and the French Fleet at his rear. On October 19, 1781, he surrendered the almost 8,000 troops under his command, and hostilities ceased. Pending a formal Peace Treaty, Washington kept the Continental Army headquartered at New Windsor, New York. He and his good friend George Clinton took a three-week trip through the New York frontier looking for land to buy. They eventually purchased 6,071 acres south of Utica where the Village of New Hartford is now located. The Treaty of Paris was signed on September 9, 1783, but the British did not leave New York City until November 25 of that year.

Governor Clinton now turned to peacetime problems, the attempt of the restless Green Mountain Boys to separate Vermont, the proposed confiscation of the property of the Loyalists and the frontier raids. In addition, he had to clear title to central New York State. To perfect title to the most easterly part, on June 28, 1785, the Governor signed a Treaty with the remnants of the Oneida and Tuscarora tribes. Under it, for $11,000 in money, trinkets and other goods, they were required to cede much land to the State. Next on September 12, 1788, he signed the Treaty of Fort Stanwix with the Onondaga tribe and on February 25, 1789, he signed the Treaty of Albany with the Cayuga tribe. Thus title to the Town of Fayette was cleared and to the west of it title to the two million acres in central New York State promised to veterans of the Revolutionary War. This was called the Military Tract. In each case reservations were made for the native tribes who ceded this land.

As a first step in developing these ceded lands, the State's Surveyor General surveyed the town of Fayette, later divided into the towns of Oxford and Guilford. The town of Fayette was divided into 100 Lots, each containing 640 acres (a square mile) more or less. All these surveyed Lots were between the Unadilla River on the east and the Chenango River on the west. A triangular piece, known as the Gore, was west of the Chenango.

Under the State Constitution, the State Land Commission on which the Governor sat, had the power to grant Patents (title) to vacant or waste land east of the Military Tract. Some Patents were sold at public auction for cash. Others were granted to applicants on the condition they would make settlements within a limited number of years. Melancton Smith, a friend and political backer of Governor Clinton, was one of the first to be granted Patents in Fayette. In September 1786 he was granted Patents for four lots, a total of 2,864 acres, adjacent to the Unadilla River on condition they be settled in seven years. Settling these new lots benefited the state in three ways. The amount paid for the land auctioned enriched the state's treasury, there were new landowners on whom to impose real property taxes and the settlers prevented the native tribes from reclaiming their former hunting grounds.

Many land speculators urged the Governor to build a road across the Southern Tier. By way of background, Nancy Isenberg, in her heralded biography of Aaron Burr, *Fallen Founder,* recounts a land deal south of the site of Oxford. She says: "Burr's own family had their sights set on land in New York State. His three maternal uncles — Timothy Edwards, Jonathan Edwards, Jr. and Pierpont Edwards — drew their nephew into various ventures. One of the most important was the Boston Ten Townships in New York's Southern Tier, just north of the Susquehanna River, along the boundary with Pennsylvania. This portion of New York was a contested domain. Massachusetts had claims to millions of acres in what is now western New York. In 1786, a two- state commission (on which Burr's uncle Timothy sat) reached an agreement by which Massachusetts gained full preemptive rights to lands between the Oswego (sic)[1]* and Chenango Rivers and west of a line drawn from Lake Ontario to the boundary with Pennsylvania. New York retained sovereignty over the vast territory, but Massachusetts could make treaties with Indians to purchase lands. Before the ink was dry on the agreement, Timothy and Jonathan Junior were negotiating to buy 230,400 acres from the Indians on the Chenango, using a land company known as the Ten Townships."

"Controversy plagued the adventure, especially when it came to apportioning the land among the investors. ... Land deals, debt and illegitimacy were the invisible threads binding Burr's extended family."[45]

The father of these three free wheeling and dealing uncles was far removed from land deals; he was Jonathan Edwards, the famous cleric, who ministered to Native Americans at Stockbridge in western Massachusetts. There, one of his boys learned to speak both the Mohawk and Mahican languages better than English at an early age

---

1   * The Owego River or Creek must have been intended. The Oswego River flows northwest by north from the vicinity of Syracuse to Lake Ontario; easily confused with the Owego Creek in Tioga County or the Otego River in Otsego County.

CHAPTER SEVEN

The Road to Fort Hill

Ox carts may pass each other with safety

Meanwhile, back in New England, Benjamin Hovey continued to perform his foraging for the Continental Army and his duties for the Sherriff of Worcester so well that as the Revolution ended in 1782, Chandler appointed Benjamin to the position of a full-fledged Deputy Sheriff. Celebrating this promotion, Lydia brought forth a son, Alfred, the next year. Although only 24, Benjamin had to carry out the many duties of the sheriff, who was the principal executive officer of the County. Under Provincial Law, the Sheriff was entitled to 25 percent of the poundage (statutory fees) collected by Deputy Sheriffs. Thus, the appointment showed the sheriff had faith in Benjamin's honesty and integrity. The duties which the sheriff delegated to his deputy included enforcing the laws; quelling riots; caring for and disciplining prisoners; serving writs, subpoenas and other legal process; foreclosing mortgages; and even calling out the militia. The poundage from these endeavors helped Benjamin provide for his growing family. Perhaps even more important for his future career, was the practical "know-how" he gained in conveyances and other land transactions.

Benjamin continued to serve as Deputy Sheriff for four years. During that time, Nancy was born in 1784. In 1786, he began his final military service for Massachusetts. This was during Shays' Rebellion. Daniel Shays, son of Irish immigrants, was a farm hand. At the beginning of the Revolutionary War, he enlisted in the local militia as a private, fought at Bunker Hill, and with great distinction in the Battle of Saratoga. He rose to become a captain in the Fifth Massachusetts Regiment. After five years of service he returned to farming. The Continental Congress had little means to pay the Army. That obligation for the most part fell on the newly formed States. Instead of cash, many officers received their overdue stipend in grants of land suitable for farming. Before the War this had been a profitable enterprise. Despite the seemingly favorable Treaty of Paris signed on December 9, 1783, by John Adams, John Jay and Benjamin Franklin for America and David Hadley for Britain, the British closed the lucrative West Indian ports to Yankee shipping, claiming that America had not restored property taken from the Tories as the Treaty required. Thus trade declined to a fraction of its former amount, bringing on what was called the Depression of 1786. The taxes on farmers were increased by state legislatures to pay off the war debts. Furthermore the taxes had to be paid in hard currency, gold or silver metal coins, rather than paper money "not worth a Continental." In fact, according to the noted historian, Kenneth C. Davis, "a strapped Daniel Shays had been forced to give up a prized possession. Shays had paid off a twelve-dollar debt by selling the famous gold-handled ceremonial sword that had been presented to him by the Marquis de Lafayette in honor of the victory at Saratoga."[46] There was a dearth of such metal specie and when taxes were not paid, Sheriffs placed red flags on houses to signal an impending auction. With two hundred hard-luck men facing foreclosure, the Shaysites, led by Job Shattuck, marched on, surrounded and shut down the Courts. The Courts in those days had, in addition to judicial powers, both legislative and executive powers, so their closing was tantamount to shutting down the Massachusetts government.

By January 1787, the situation had become critical. Many militiamen sympathized with the Shaysites. Since Congress would do nothing, Massachusetts Governor James Bowdoin had to raise a private army. Benjamin Hovey again volunteered, and now a Lieutenant, marched to Springfield under the command of the grossly obese General Benjamin Lincoln. He was best or rather worst known for his lack of success in defending Charleston and Savannah in 1779. This time he was successful. His force reached the Springfield Armory just before some 1,200 Shaysites could rifle it. The rebels were repulsed by artillery on January 25, 1787. Four were killed and others wounded. By February 27, the revolt was quelled (see page 176) and the troops returned to their homes.

Perhaps the most famous image of Shay's Rebellion: "Regulators" Daniel Shays (left) and Job Shattuck (right), from a 1787 Boston Almanack woodcut, Artist unknown.

The revolt had a far-reaching effect. In London, it stirred American Ambassador John Adams to write a treatise on *A Defense of the Constitution of Governments*. In this treatise he emphasized: "If there is one central truth to be collected from the history of all ages, it is this: that the people's rights and liberties, and the democratical mixture of a constitution, can never be preserved without a strong executive, or, in other words, without separating the executive from the legislative power."[47] This central truth certainly applied to the defeat of the Iroquois Nation.

This idea was embodied in the Federal Constitution adopted on September 17, 1787, at the Constitutional Convention in Philadelphia. It was then circulated to the States for ratification. There was strong opposition to the Constitution because it lacked a bill of rights. Many of the smaller states overlooked this. Some like Georgia, then on the frontier, needed the protection afforded by a strong central government. Moreover the smaller states were represented by as many senators as the large states. James Madison of Virginia, author of much of the Constitution, aided by New Yorkers, Alexander Hamilton and John Jay, developed a strategy of getting the smaller states to ratify it first and five did so quickly. However, in the major states of Massachusetts, New York and Virginia, many anti-federalists opposed it. In Virginia Patrick Henry, of "give me liberty or give me death" fame, declaimed it did not guarantee the liberties for which he had fought. Finally a compromise was reached in Massachusetts. In February 1788 it ratified the Constitution with the understanding Congress would consider adding a Bill of Rights. This compromise led to five more states ratifying the Constitution and thereafter the Bill of Rights was adopted.

With the country adopting a new Constitution, Benjamin Hovey took a new lease on life. He had worked for the Sheriff of Worcester County, the largest county in Massachusetts, since he was a teenager. His promotion to a full-fledged Deputy at age 24 in 1782 brought in more poundage, but in addition to Ruth, Alphena, Alfred, and Nancy, Mary was born in 1787. With four daughters and a son to support, he had to earn more. He also had a large circle of friends, whom, according to the *Annals of Oxford*, he entertained at his own expense, indeed more lavishly than his purse could bear. His earnings from the sheriff's office had been supplemented by some farm income, but the British blockade of trade with the West Indies following the end of the Revolutionary War affected all farmers adversely. So setting aside the security of a lean to modest living in Massachusetts, Benjamin set out for the west.

Benjamin left Lydia to care for the children. Ruth was and Alphena was about to become a sturdy teenager. They could help with the farm chores and Alfred and Nancy were old enough to help care for the toddler Mary. Benjamin crossed the Hudson and thence down the Susquehanna River to Unadilla, New York, a small village about 50 miles southwest of Cooperstown, just west of the Catskill Mountains. It is located at the confluence of the Unadilla and Susquehanna Rivers. He bought a nearby farm of 283 acres.

The Secretary of State advertised in newspapers that proposals would be received for exploring, laying out and completing roads.[48] It seems probable that Benjamin answered such an advertisement for he received a commission to build the first road from the Unadilla to the Chenango River. To do so, Benjamin first reconnoitered the route from his farm near Unadilla to the Chenango River. He learned that the Chenango River is ninety miles long and for most of its length is navigable by canoe. It arises about 20 miles west of present-day Utica, New York, and draining surrounding hills, flows south to Norwich where it turns southwest and flows through Oxford to Greene where it is joined by the Tioughnioga River. From there it winds its sinuous way to Binghamton where it joins the Susquehanna.

He found the country through which the Chenango flows was largely forested by hemlock, oak, pine and a prickly thistle called chenango by the Indians with some patches of northern hardwoods, such as ash on well watered slopes, and beech, birch, black cherry, chestnut, elm and hard and soft maples with some sycamores and striped maple in wet areas. Although we may be sure the selling Oneida and Tuscarora tribes had harvested most of the beavers for their valuable pelts, there was still much other game. The successful hunters sometimes dined on such birds as ruffed grouse and wild turkeys (or feasted on passenger pigeons on the rare occasions when they passed by in the thousands) and on such game as white-tail deer, varying hare, martens, mink, opossums, otters, porcupines, raccoons, grey squirrels, or if really starving, even red squirrels and chipmunks. They also shot predators, including bob-cats, wolves and rarely a panther.

Benjamin laid out the first portion of the road that would ultimately reach Lake Cayuga. It followed in part an old military trail from Unadilla to the Chenango River, a distance of above 20 miles. At this juncture the Chenango Valley was more than a mile wide, with most of the floor lying east of the river, an ideal site for a town. Benjamin led and worked on a building crew that included Francis Balcom, Solomon Dodge and Thomas and James McAlpine. This crew really made the chips fly as they cut the road through forests. In addition to axes, two man saws, picks and shovels, there were oxen to draw metal or wooden scrapers. Provisions for the crew were brought up the river by canoe from Tioga Point, Pennsylvania.

This road transverses the 100 lots in the township of Fayette surveyed by the State's Surveyor General. Benjamin Hovey acquired title to Lot 92, on the east bank of the Chenango

River, which is now the site of the eastern portion of the Town of Oxford. He acquired 428 of these acres from David Baites and his wife Molly by deed not dated until June 18, 1792, for 480 pounds, lawful money of the State of New York. From correspondence from an attorney of that time, we know Hovey was acting at least in part with unnamed proprietors for whom he was the land agent. We know that after Melancton Smith died of yellow fever in 1792, Benjamin Hovey acknowledged that the land he still owned in Lot 92 was owed as a tenant in common with Melancton Smith.

When he reached the east bank of the Chenango River late in the fall of 1790, Benjamin found a small hill, or perhaps better described as a large mound, about two and one-half acres in area. It was a semi-circle, the flat side of about 240 yards being the east bank of the river. Around the outside was a four-foot ditch, providing a first line of defense. At the southern end of Fort Hill, Benjamin found decaying wooden and earthen breast works from two to three yards in thickness, providing a second line of defense. This final fort had not been used for some years for it was now thickly covered with second growth beach and maple trees.

Later Benjamin heard many tales about Fort Hill from friendly Indians in the vicinity, no two of which were exactly alike. From these and other sources it now appears that a small remnant of the Susquehanna tribe, called the Antones, had migrated to Fort Hill, a traditional hunting ground of the Oneidas. This tribe was headed by the great warrior, Thick Neck. He was so strong he could shoot arrows with a bow that few others could even bend. The Oneidas sent out a peace party to parley with Thick Neck, but it was captured and tortured to death. Next the Oneidas sent out a war party, but it too was ambushed and slaughtered.

To do away with Thick Neck once and for all, the Oneidas, together with the best warriors from their allies, the Senecas, assembled a larger war party. Rather than attack Thick Neck on Fort Hill, they waited until he had gone hunting outside the fort. He was then attacked and wounded by flights of arrows as thick as rain. Though bloody, he fled to Lake Warn, grabbed a reed to breathe through and hid himself under the water, but drops of blood gave away his subterranean whereabouts. He was captured, killed and buried on its banks. His family and followers were adopted by the Oneidas.

So, thankfully when Benjamin arrived at Fort Hill, Thick Neck was long gone, but Benjamin was not the first white settler. There were already two squatters, Elijah Blackman and his friend, James Phelps. Phelps soon moved away but returned several years later. The other, Elijah Blackman lived on an island in the river. Showing his unusual gift for tact, rather than summarily ousting Blackman from his illegal perch, Benjamin made an ally instead of a potential enemy. By making an allowance for the improvements on the island made by Blackman, Benjamin persuaded Blackman to purchase one of the lots up the river. Thus, although Elijah Blackman had arrived first, Benjamin Hovey was the first lawful settler of the town to which he subsequently gave the name Oxford for his former Massachusetts home. He cut the first tree to clear the ground where the village was to be built.

In his booklet, *Some Early Settlers of Oxford Before 1800*, the Reverend Roland A. Boutwell, who knew Blackman, sets forth his understanding of his meeting with Hovey:

"During one of the brisk November days, Blackman was outside his cabin chopping wood. He stopped to wipe his brow. Suddenly, with gaping mouth, he looked towards the shore. To his amazement he saw a man standing there, a broad grin lighting up his friendly face.

Our imagination will have to reconstruct the conversation that might have followed.

> *Blackman:* Say now, but it sure is good to see a new face around here. My name is Elijah Blackman, Why don't you come across the bridge and set for a spell.
>
> *Hovey:* Many thanks, Mr. Blackman. By the way, my name is Benjamin Hovey. I'm from the town of Oxford, back in Massachusetts.

Hovey crossed to the island. Immediately he was engulfed by the Blackman family, all anxious to shake his hand and get news from the outside world. They invited him into their cabin, prepared and ate a simple meal, after which Hovey and Blackman took a walk.

> *Blackman:* You aimin' to settle down in these parts, Mr. Hovey?
>
> *Hovey:* Well, as a matter of fact, I am. The thing of it is, I own this land.
>
> *Blackman:* Do you, now? A'int that just my luck? How much of the land do you own around here?
>
> *Hovey:* Oh, somewhere in the neighborhood of 7,000 acres.
>
> *Blackman:* Do tell. That's a heap of land for one man. What are you goin' to do with it all?
>
> *Hovey:* If the good Lord is willing, I'm going to build a new town up and down the banks of

this river. I've been thinking about it for quite a spell.

Blackman: Well, that sure is a good ambition. What made you decide to do a thing like that?

Hovey: When I was helping to send the Red Coats back to England where they belong, I decided that someday, I was going to do something about helping to settle a new part of this great country of ours, once it belonged to us, and not that old Devil of a King George. Well, sir, when the war was done with, I went back to my home. Things began to get a little rough for me, financially, that is. So I decided that now was as good a time as any to do what I had been dreaming about. So here I am. I've been commissioned to build a road from Unadilla to Cayuga Lake. Just as soon as I get my cabin built, I want to get the project started. You got any good ideas for a spot to build a cabin on?

Blackman: Matter of fact, I have. Not far from here up above the river bank, there's an old fort that must have belonged to the Indians. Right near there is a good place to build. It gives you a good view of what's goin' and comin' down the river.

But I'd like to ask you about my wife and family. Seein' as you own this land you'll probably want us movin' on. Do you mind if we winter it out here, and then, come spring, we'll be movin' to some other spot?

Hovey: Listen, my friend, I've got no objection to your staying here permanently. But I think you made a poor choice by setting down on an island. Come spring, you're likely to be floating down the river. Besides you have cleared a spot there on the island. I'd call that improving my land. If you'll give me a hand building a cabin, I'll give you a few acres of your own choice. What do you say?

Blackman and Hovey shook hands on it.

That first winter, with Blackman's help, Benjamin made a dugout hut at the northern end of Fort Hill from which one could see up and down the river. The hut had a facing of several logs, one from the first tree cut to make the village, and some stones piled for a temporary chimney. Greased paper made a window and an old blanket, the door. He survived his first winter at Oxford on a diet of dried apples and corn, supplemented occasionally by deer meat and fish from the river.[49] With the help of Solomon Dodge, he improved his hut enough to bring his family to it in 1791. At that time it consisted of Lydia who was 36, Ruth 16, Alphena 13, Alfred 8, Nancy, barely 7 and little Mary, 4 years old. Otis, who became a portrait painter, and Samuel who died at an early age, were born after the move.

And what a move it was; beyond 250 miles, with need for preserving food for the long isolated winter ahead. There were no apple orchards within a day's canoe trip from Oxford, New York. So we may assume they prepared for the move in a sensible way. It made sense to organize a giant paring bee before leaving Massachusetts. Hundreds of bushels of apples were picked. With friends and neighbors from miles around, they were pared and quartered. In fact, the Hovey girls were so deft at the art of paring that their techniques were handed down through generations.

The pared apples were placed on drying racks. The seeds of the apples were placed on the hot bricks in the fireplace and watched until they popped for either a good or bad omen. "An unbroken paring was waved three times around the head then dropped to the floor, and the letter it formed was the first in the name of the future wife or husband."[50] When the pared apples were all on the drying racks, a sumptuous supper was served followed by dancing and games.

The Hovey family likely left their Massachusetts home on an October day when the leaves were like an artist's palette of colors hung on the trees. The trip across Massachusetts could be made by stagecoach, with several trunks of household items. After a ferryboat trip across the Hudson River, there were more than 150 miles to travel in New York beyond stagecoach service. Travel by ox cart was slow and wearisome, but the family reached the enlarged hut at Fort Hill late in the fall of 1791. There the dark coniferous trees must at first seemed dismal, but Benjamin, who may have met the family in Unadilla, likely sent one of the older girls to teach Alfred how to fish in the Chenango. There is nothing more satisfying than the praise received for bringing home a good catch of trout or bass for supper, except perhaps eating that catch.

According to a granddaughter living in Syracuse, "They chose with taste as the Chenango River passes through the town. Grandfather's log hut was directly on its banks. There they fought the Indians, went forty miles to a mill in a canoe and to Onondaga County for salt, and had a pioneer life, but men were men in those days true to their time."

This granddaughter exaggerates the fighting with the Indians. Of course, not every member of the Oneida nation was a party to or approved of the 1785 sale of these lands by their chiefs. The Chenango land was mostly a terminal coniferous forest, traditionally used by the Indians only as hunting grounds in the fall. As it was cleared for farming the felled tree- tops and edge of fields provided plenty of browse, the favorite food of white-tail deer, and their herds increased — as did the packs of wolves. In fact, the wolves became so numerous that at the Town Meeting held in 1796 it was voted to "give four pounds for each wolf's pate killed in this Town." The early settlers did not interfere with these Indian hunting parties, indeed some welcomed them and were rewarded with a hind quarter or two of venison for their hospitality. A few Indians stayed near the white settlements for many years, hunting, fishing and making baskets and brooms for sale.

Besides Benjamin's family, a number of young men came to Oxford in 1791. By 1792, the population of Oxford and adjacent areas of Tioga County had increased to the extent that Governor Clinton, aware of the Indian threat and confident of the leadership qualities of Benjamin Hovey, advised the Council on Appointments that he wished to arrange the militia of Tioga County into one regiment and two battalions. The Council, consisting of Phillip Van Cortlandt, Daniel Pye, William Powers and Stephen Van Rensselaer appointed Benjamin Hovey, Major Commandant of a Battalion on March 3, 1792.[51]

One of the young men arriving in 1791 was Uri Tracy, a graduate of Yale College in the class of 1789. He was a Presbyterian minister sent as a missionary to the Indians. Two years later, on August 28, 1793, he married Ruth, the Hovey's' eldest daughter. With a minister as a son-in-law, Benjamin and Lydia saw no need to found a Universalist Church in Oxford.

Others who arrived in 1791 were Francis Balcom and Solomon Dodge, members of the road crew. Balcom had met Benjamin Hovey in Unadilla, and like him, had not had much education. Accordingly, to complete his education, he helped to build, and though 27 years old, attended the Oxford Academy when it opened.

Now that the road replacing the military trail from Unadilla to Oxford was complete, Benjamin undertook to extend it. In 1791 he submitted the following proposal to the Land Commissioners.

"The subscriber Benjamin Hovey of Otsego County Yeoman Doth hereby contract with the said [Land] Commissioners to explore and lay out a Road from where the Road laid out by him last year under the direction of the said Commissioners meets the Chenango River to the East Boundary of the Township named Cincinnatus in the lands laid out for the use of the Army and to open and clear same of trees logs and underwood of such width that Sleighs Carts and Wagons may conveniently pass, and to make Bridges over such small streams and gullies as otherwise cannot be conveniently passed, and causeway such many places as it would be impracticable to pass without them, and so level the side hills that Sleighs and Wagons may safely pass along. In consideration thereof the said Commissioners shall grant to the Subscriber the quantity of twenty five hundred acres of land on Oneida Lake, which has been set apart in virtue of a Law for Opening Roads on the Subscribers producing to the said Commissioners the Surveyors Generals Certificate or other satisfactory Proof that the said Road is made and Complete agreeable to the Tenor of this Contract.

"Given under my hand this first day of April in the year of Our Lord One Thousand Seven Hundred and Ninety One.— Note the Road to be completed agreeable to the Tenor of this Contract in Eighteen Months. /s/ Benj. Hovey"

This contract shows that Benjamin had learned to write and even prepare a contract, but the deficiency in punctuation highlights his lack of education.

Benjamin was able to complete the road before the end of the year. On the 6th of January 1792, Solomon Martin, David Baits and seven others attested that two ox carts could pass on it. In due course the State conveyed 5,000 acres to Hovey located in the "Road" Township in Herkimer County near Lake Oneida. He promptly sold these acres for 40 cents per acre, a total of $2,000.

The road extended west from Oxford about fourteen miles to the Township of Cincinnatus on the eastern border of what is now Cortland County, then mostly part of the Military Tract, reserved for grants to Revolutionary War soldiers, who had been promised land in lieu of pay. Most of them sold their land warrants rather than move into an uncharted wilderness.

In the fall of 1792, John Lincklaen, a surveyor for the Holland Land Company, left Kingston, New York, to survey 20 townships in the Cazenovia Tract in which the Holland Land Company had an interest. He came west along the Esopus River past Shandaken through the Blue [Catskill] Mountains. After a journey of three days he reached Oxford on October 3, 1792. Hovey welcomed a chance to meet someone representing the well-financed Dutch syndicate. As Oxford had no Inn as yet, Hovey must have told his son Alfred to camp out for a few nights to make room for Lincklaen. He stayed with Hovey for three days and learned much about the Townships he was to survey, but let him tell it through his own notes.

"11. Mr. Hovey pays 3 pounds, 10 shillings for clearing an acre, and the men who do the work have the ashes, for which he gives 6 pence per bushel.

12. Mr. Hovey has 2000 acres [already committed] to sell in the Township no. 11. He could let us have 8000 acres there.

13. The contracts that he has made with Messrs. Watkins & Flint to survey their lands, are that they pay him 20 shillings per mile, then he is responsible for all the expenses and sends the owners the survey, a map and a fieldbook. But as our lands are more in the neighborhood he will undertake to make the contract for less than 20 shill. The surveyor whom he employs is named Lock [Nathaniel Locke, who later married, Mary, Benjamin and Lydia's youngest daughter], who earns from 10 to 16 shill. per day.

14. To cut the road from Hovey's to Cayuga Lake, they pay 10 pounds per acre: the contractors must then cut it 2 rods wide, and make necessary bridges. A wood road where a cart can pass costs 2 pounds per mile.

15. The surveyors employed by Mr. Hovey are Nath. Lock of Westchester County & Walter Sabin who lives on the Susqueh.: near J: Mercereau: each surveyor has with 5 hands, 2 Chainmen 2 markmen & 1 to carry the provisions.—The surveyor when running the outlines is allowed 2 Dlrs. a day, when Lotting out 12 shill. a day. W. Sabin runs commonly 5 or 6 miles a day. N. Lock 8—10 miles a day. Lock's hands have 10 Dlrs. a month. Sabin's hands have only 8 Dlrs. a month. Each hand is allowed a day 2 pounds of Beef or 1-1/2 pound of pork, 2 pounds of bread, & as much Chocolate or Tea as they can drink, as much Rum as they will carry, each party takes generally a Cask containing 5 Gallons. We'll reckon that each man is allowed a gill [1/4 pint] a day. Hovey buys a yoke of oxen (2 oxen) for 16 to 20 pounds & the pork

5 Dlrs. a hundred weight; he sells the pork at a shill. a pound & the beef 5 pence a pound.

Each man that goes in the woods carries for a fortnight or 20 days provisions that is from 70 to 80 weight, he walks then from 15 to 20 miles a day."

Lincklaen goes on to describe property owned by a Col. Smith. (This was William Stephens Smith, who graduated from Princeton in 1774, served as an aide to Washington, Von Steuben, and Lafayette, rising to the rank of Colonel. Then as Adjutant General under General John Sullivan during the expedition that defeated the Senecas near Elmira in 1779, he became familiar with the Chenango region. Later in London he married the daughter of John Adams named for her mother, Abigail Amelia.)

Lincklaen gives a rundown by Mr. Hovey of the 20 Townships in which the Holland Land Company had an interest and gives details of a sale by Hovey of 5,000 acres for $2,812 (about 56 cents an acre) these apparently being land he received for road building. Finally he includes in his expense account:

Oct. 5:	[pounds, shillings and pence]
Mr. Hovey for 20 lb. beef	5 – 8 – 4
10 lb. bacon 1 S lb.	10
2 lb. sugar	2
1/2 lb. tea	2 – 6
Board & Lodging	17 – 2
Baking Bread	4
For Washing	3 – 6

Then, later on Oct. 20:

Hovey's man 16 day's service:
At 4/6 a day is 3 -12.

It is obvious Hovey was very forthcoming with information for this agent of the Holland Land Company, but he was vitally interested in its properties and plans, and in the three days he boarded Lincklaen he learned a lot. The Holland Land Company had been organized by a Dutch syndicate in Holland to buy lands in New York. Since at that time aliens could not own land in that state, it worked through trustees and a general agent, Theopile Cazenove, for whom Cazenovia, New York, was later named. Although most famous for buying hundreds of thousands of acres west of the Genesee river, its first purchases known as the Lincklaen or Cazenovia tract were north and west of Oxford. This tract was about seven miles wide and twenty miles long and was surveyed by Nathaniel Locke into lots supposed to contain 150 acres.

Lincklaen's notes show that by this time Hovey had given up trying to do everything himself. He now functioned as a general contractor for surveying, road building and other projects.

In its early days Hovey opened Oxford's first store. He soon took in his son-in-law Uri Tracy as a partner but they were both too busy to give store keeping proper attention and hired Asatel Rockwell as a clerk. It appears Rockwell entered into unauthorized transactions in the name of the partnership. Accordingly, they placed a notice in the *Catskill Packet* on April 11, 1785, stating that they would not be responsible for any of his engagements on their behalf.[52] Soon Samuel Farnham opened a separate store and is given credit for being Oxford's first storekeeper.[53]

In addition to storekeeping, land deals, surveying and road building, Hovey was engaged in the building of the Village. This also involved surveying lots and laying out parks. He became the leading man of the region. Those who knew him reported that he was a man of strong common sense and vigor in action and had other personal qualities necessary for the arduous labor and hardships of pioneer life.

Meanwhile, Melancton Smith and General Marinus Willett were busy purchasing land on the western side of the Chenango from the state. Smith was born in 1724 and educated at his families' dinner table. He served in the Continental Congress in 1785 and 1786 and later in the New York legislature. As a leading anti-federalist, at the New York Convention to consider the adoption of the federal Constitution, he was the principal debater opposed to its adoption. As Chancellor Kent observed, "Smith was noted for his love of reading, his tenacious memory, powerful intellect and for the metaphysical and logical discussion of which he was master."

His principal opponent was Alexander Hamilton, author of many of the *Federalist Papers*. Hamilton and Smith had formerly been closely allied as opponents of slavery, which was not outlawed in New York until 1800, but now Smith felt too much power was vested in the federal government.

Before the final vote, news reached the Convention that the eighth and ninth states had ratified the Constitution. This satisfied the condition that the Constitution would go into effect if ratified by nine states. The issue was no longer whether it was sound idea, but whether New York would or would not be part of the United States of America. After Virginia also ratified the Constitution, Smith changed sides, and by a margin of three votes, New York ratified the Constitution in 1783. Smith was then appointed Sheriff of Duchess County. Later he went into business in New York City.

Brigadier General Marinus Willett joined with Smith in a number of land deals. Willett is best known for saving Fort Stanwix in the Mohawk Valley. It had been surrounded by British and Indian forces under the command of Colonel Barrimore St.

Ledger. Disguised as a Tory (and so risking death if caught as a spy) he escaped through enemy lines and led Continental forces to save the Fort and force St. Ledger to retreat to Canada. This eliminated the western threat and helped defeat British General John Burgoyne in the pivotal Battle of Saratoga in October 1777. (Later Marinus Willett, after he became Mayor of New York City in 1808, is also worst known by the epithet, the badass Mayor.)

Willett like Smith was a leading anti-federalist politician. As such, he and Smith had backed George Clinton's successful runs for Governor of New York. They then applied to the land office for the tract of land on the western side of the Chenango River known as the Gore.[54] The Gore comprised 7,046 acres. The Land Office approved its sale to Smith and Willett for four shillings and

General Marinus Willett (July 31, 1740 – August 22, 1830).

one pence per acre. Smith assigned his interest to Willett who paid the entire purchase price. On December 12, 1792, Governor George Clinton conveyed the Gore to Willett on condition that within seven years "there shall be one family actually settled on the said tract of land hereby granted, for every six hundred and forty acres thereof, otherwise these our Letters Patent and the estate hereby granted, shall cease, determine and become void."

This meant that Willett had to be sure that the Gore was occupied by at least 12 families within seven years. Willett sold almost half of the lots he had just purchased to Benjamin Hovey for just a fraction more than his cost. Willett need not have worried with Benjamin on the job as land agent. Or was it his hospitable wife or four pretty daughters? By 1792, only two years after the building of the first log hut, James A. Glover (not the James Glover that later married Alphena Hovey) established a grist mill in nearby Preston eliminating the canoe trip to Unadilla to grind corn and grain. By 1795 the census reported 150 heads of families, a miraculous immigration to Oxford.

CHAPTER EIGHT

Founding Oxford, New York

The Heyday of Land Speculation?

There have been a number of notorious land booms in the United States. Perhaps the most famous is the Oklahoma Land Rush. At high noon on April 22, 1889, the "boomers," an estimated 50,000 of them, many in wagons with whips ready to crack, others astride a swift and sturdy steed with saddlebags filled and spurs sharpened, pawing the official starting line, awaited the starting boom. At one entrance the boom was the clarion call of a cavalry bugle, at another the sharp report of a rifle shot, and, living up to its name, at another the boom of a cannon. At the boom the whips cracked, the spurs dug in and they were off to claim the most attractive of the 12,500 lots available, each comprising 160 acres, only to be shocked to find they were preceded by a "sooner" who had jumped the official starting line by days or weeks. Years of title disputes and litigation followed.

A more recent example is the land boom mostly on Florida's west coast commencing in the 1950s. With the development of residential air-conditioning in Tampa in 1935, Florida, which had always attracted snowbirds that could not take the cold, now also became bearable for rugged, hardy individuals who could not take the heat. The three Mackle Brothers and two Rosen Brothers, all great salesmen, sparked the creation of such major corporations as General Development Corporation, Gulf American Corporation and Deltona Corporation, among others. Lots were sold for a pittance down, followed by installments over five or even ten or more years. In addition to traditional advertising in print media throughout the World, American customers were attracted by free steak dinners and offers to fly free on captive airlines to see their future retirement home.

With inadequate or non-existent record keeping, sometimes a Purchase Contract for an attractive lot was signed with two or even three different buyers and the matter left uncorrected, hoping for early or late "burn off" (forfeiture for failure to pay installments on time) until the day it came to convey title. Solicitors in telephone boiler rooms ran up millions of dollars of charges every year trying to keep "lonely hearts" paying their installments. Purchase Contracts failed to disclose that some lots were underwater from time to time or indeed most of the time. Also it was not disclosed that they lacked water or septic systems. In some cases regulations prevented installing wells because of nearby septic tanks or the converse, regulations prevented installing septic tanks because of nearby wells. In the early days of some of these projects, it was not uncommon whenever there were three lot holders in a row for the middle lot holder to build his house first with a well and a septic tank making the other two lots useless until municipal water and sewer became available. It was not until 1968 that Congress regulated [55] interstate land sales by vendors of multiple lots in an attempt to stop such fraud and abuse.

But these recent examples were certainly eclipsed by the gigantic grants and sales of lands by New York State. Excluding the land ceded to Massachusetts by Treaty, these were made by the New York Land Commission, chaired and controlled by Governor George Clinton. For example, the Land Commission, on which both New York Governor George Clinton and Attorney General Aaron Burr served, sold 500,000 acres to John and Nicholas Roosevelt for 18 cents an acre. Overcoming a resolution of censure in 1791, Assemblyman Melancton Smith, introduced a resolution approving the conduct of the Commissioners, which was passed.

The document making the grant by the government was called a Patent rather than a deed. The Governor was not afraid of blowing his own horn — or was it the Attorney General, Aaron Burr, trying to curry favor — for the printed form of these Patents wound up with this rodomontade:

> "**WITNESS** our Truly and Well beloved GEORGE CLINTON, Esquire, Governor of our said State, General and Commander in Chief of all the Militia, and Admiral of the Navy of the same, ..."

Some of these Patents were auctioned off to the highest bidders, but many conveying lots in the town of Fayette were granted by the state without charge, but subject to the condition that there be an actual settlement within a term of years, usually seven, or the lot would revert to the state. The seven year condition was set forth in four Patents granted to Melancton Smith in September 1786, the eleventh year of Independence. These four Patents, each for 640 acres, were along the eastern boundary of the town of Fayette adjacent to the Unadilla River.

Eventually, Benjamin Hovey was able to buy out most of the land originally acquired by both Melancton Smith and Marinus Willett on both sides of the Chenango. They had to raise money because they became liable on a surety bond. They had agreed to be sureties in the amount of $50,000 for General John Lamb, when he had become collector of customs for the Port of New York. In 1796, it was discovered that one of his employees had embezzled $150,000 for which he was liable, as were his sureties to the extent of their $50,000 bond.

Hovey is mentioned in a letter from Samuel Miles Hopkins to a friend. At age 21, Hopkins was admitted to the New York Bar in New York City on motion of Aaron Burr. Burr recommended he begin the practice of law in Tioga County where he could certainly earn $52 in the first year and could live on a dollar a week. With $10.25 in cash, a valise, clothes, and a set of Blackstone law tomes, Hopkins set forth on his horse, Phoenix. He describes his migration to Oxford in the letter, which was read to the Oxford Academy Jubilee 50 years after the Academy was founded in 1794. It follows:

"Over one hundred ten miles west from Catskill, through a country almost entirely new, brought me to the village of Oxford and to the house of Benjamin Hovey, the founder of it, and who had eighteen months before cut the first tree to clear the ground where the village stood. Here too I found Uri Tracy (of a class in [Yale] College two years older than myself) and whom after forty years I still count among the most valuable of my friends. Here I took my residence. Hovey was a man of very strong natural sense and vigor of action but very little education. He had been unfortunate in Massachusetts. His family had preserved life in the wilderness for some days by eating the grain from the ear in an unripe state. Suddenly he started to New York, laid open plans for the settlement of lands to the proprietors, whom he found, built Oxford on his own lands and became the leading man of a very growing country. I settled in Oxford as a lawyer. My first law draft I made by writing on the head of a barrel, under a roof made of poles only, and in the rain, which I kept partially from spattering my paper, by a broad-brimmed hat. In such a village as this, the first framed building was an academy, of two stories high, and Mr. Tracy was the teacher. No Yankees without the means of education."[56]

This letter refers to Hovey laying out his plans "to the proprietors whom he found" yet it also states "he built Oxford on his own land." It was of course his own land of record, but the many references to him as land agent lead us to believe he was acting for others. This enigma, perhaps stemming from the fire that destroyed many state records, has led us on a four-year trail to the counties of Montgomery, Herkimer and Tioga and to the State Archives in Albany. We have learned that Hovey did not start out with all of Lot 192, the lot in which all of Oxford east of the Chenango is located. As previously mentioned on June 8, 1792, Hovey purchased 428 acres of Lot 192 from David Baites and Molly, his wife, who signed the deed with an X, for the sum of 180 pounds lawful money of the State of New York.

It seems someone had helped Hovey acquire the square mile in his own name. Besides Melancton Smith and Marinus Willett, who could it have been? Could it have been Aaron Burr and the Edwards brothers? That seems unlikely. They were busy acquiring the "Boston Ten Townships" to the south, along the border of Pennsylvania between the Chenango and Otego Rivers. Could it have been Colonel William Stephens Smith, the son-in-law of John Adams, the Vice President? He had campaigned through the Chenango region during the Revolutionary War. On returning from London, where he served as Secretary of the American legation, he began buying lands in New York. These included lands in the Oxford Township that were purchased for an English Lord, William Pulteney, who as an alien, had to deal through Trustees.

Finally, could it have been Governor Clinton? Governor Clinton was reputed to be very wealthy but very frugal, almost parsimonious in his personal habits. He may have acquired part of his wealth from an interest in the land at Oxford. Hovey had showed him he was a person who got things done; road building, for one. Clinton, in each case through the Council on Appointment, first appointed Hovey as Major, commanding a Battalion[57] in the New York Militia, then in 1793 Lieutenant Colonel, commanding a Regiment[58] and finally, after ruling in his favor after a Court Martial, promoted him to Brigadier General, commanding a Brigade.[59] Clinton would not want his name to appear of record and would have used an intermediary, such as his friend, Melancton Smith, to be the party of record.

In the *Genealogical and Family History of Western New York*, by William V. Cutter, the following appears: "Stephen Lyons and his brothers bought land from Benjamin Hovey, Governor Clinton's land agent, for one shilling an acre and built a grist mill, lumber and woolen mill. He settled in Oxford in 1792 and made his home on Lyon Brook near Lyon Brook Bridge on the New York, Ogdensburg and Western RR."[60] Mr. Cutter may have had access to records that no longer exist, for his book predates the library fire.

Lending further credence to the close association of George Clinton and Benjamin Hovey is this election incident. In 1792, only two years after Hovey moved to Oxford, there was a bitter election contest between the Democratic-Republican (States Rights-Anti-Federalist) Party and the Federalist Party for Governor of New York. George Clinton, who had become New York's first Governor in 1777, wanted to be reelected for a sixth three year term. His running mate for Lieutenant Governor on the States Rights ticket was Pierre Van Cortlandt. They had strongly supported the War effort, but in 1783, after Congress passed a national tariff that adversely affected the customs collections by New York State, they became opposed to an all powerful national government.

Clinton's opponent was the brilliant King's College (Columbia) graduate, John Jay. Jay was well known as Minister to Spain, negotiator of the peace treaty with England and first Chief Justice of the Supreme Court of the United States. Jay was running with Philip Van Rensselaer on the Federalist ticket. The election ultimately depended on the results from the Federalist leaning Otsego County and the States-Rights leaning Clinton and Tioga Counties. The ballot boxes were required to be delivered by a sheriff or his deputy to a legislative committee of canvassers in New York City appointed pursuant to the New York Constitution. The Otsego ballots, however, were delivered by a sheriff whose term of office had expired. The Clinton County ballots were delivered by a person who had not been deputized. The Tioga ballots were entrusted to Benjamin Hovey, who had been duly appointed a Deputy Sheriff of that county. This must have been an extremely busy time for Benjamin. He was in the midst of felling timber, clearing land, surveying and selling lots, laying out roads and building cabins for new arrivals. But he also had business in Owego and New York City. So he traveled west fifty miles, a journey of at least two days, to Owego, the Tioga County seat. He took with him his clerk, James H. Thompson. The quickest way to Owego was by canoe down the Chenango to the Susquehanna. At Owego he heard that ballots had to be delivered to the Committee of Canvassers in New York City. The Secretary of State, Lewis A. Scott testified that he was not present when Hovey offered to carry the ballots for the Tioga Sheriff but that he later told the Secretary of State: "he was going to New York on his own behalf — that he would carry the said box — that it might be of some benefit to him, as he might draw pay for it.[61]" Further questions brought out the fact that the clerk might be only 17 or 18 years old. On the three hundred mile trip to New York City, Hovey became ill, but the ballots were successfully delivered to the Committee by his clerk.

A dispute immediately arose as to which of the ballots from the three counties were valid. In the case of the Tioga ballots Lewis A. Scott, Esq. testified he had prepared the affidavit of Hovey's clerk to the effect Hovey had delivered the ballot box to him duly sealed and he had delivered it to the Committee duly sealed. The dispute was referred to the two Senators from New York, Rufus King, a Federalist, and Aaron Burr, who in this matter sided with the States-Rights Party, as arbitrators. In lengthy legal arguments, King opined that all the ballots should be counted; Burr opined that only the Clinton County ballots should be counted. The upshot was that the committee rejected all three and Clinton became Governor again by 108 votes.

As noted above, the next year, 1793, Governor Clinton reformed the Regiment of the New York Militia in the part of Tioga County in which Oxford was located and appointed Benjamin Hovey as a Lieutenant Colonel in command of it.

Benjamin Hovey must have stayed in touch with his family in Oxford, Massachusetts. Before a regular post office was established and post rider hired, mail service was indeed a chancy business. In some places boxes were placed along the roads to be opened by passers-by. They would read the address and a note asking the passer-by to take the letter to the addressee if he happened to be going in his direction. No doubt Benjamin told his relatives of the land available in central New York. Moses, the older brother who had agreed to keep his parents in victuals, shortly came to Unadilla under unusual circumstances. These are set forth on page 149 of *The Hovey Book:* "In 1794, engaging in business, tradition relates of Mr. [Moses] Hovey that he became engaged in debt, and as imprisonment awaited him, he sped to New York State, having first deposited his clothing on the bank of the town's pond in Oxford to give the impression that he had drowned himself. Traveling westward he came after a few days to a town of large size; here a public sale of wild lands in that state was in progress. Although he had not $5 in his pocket, he made a bid on a large tract of land and to his surprise it was struck off to him. He obtained a few hours time in which to make payment, and obtained lodging in Foster's Tavern there. In the night he was awakened by some men clamoring for admission. He was alarmed, supposing that his creditors were in his pursuit, and hastily dressed himself. Just as he was about to leave the house, the landlord met him and told him that two men had arrived at the tavern, that they had intended to have been at the auction, but were detained, and that they wished to see him to know whether he wished to sell the lot that he had bid off. He replied that he might be induced to sell if he obtained a sufficient bonus for his bargain. In the morning he sold the land to them (except for a good farm he reserved to himself out of the tract) for several hundred dollars more than he had bid. The land was in the new township of Unadilla, in Otsego County, and there he afterwards lived. It is said that his house was the only one between Cooperstown and Oswego."

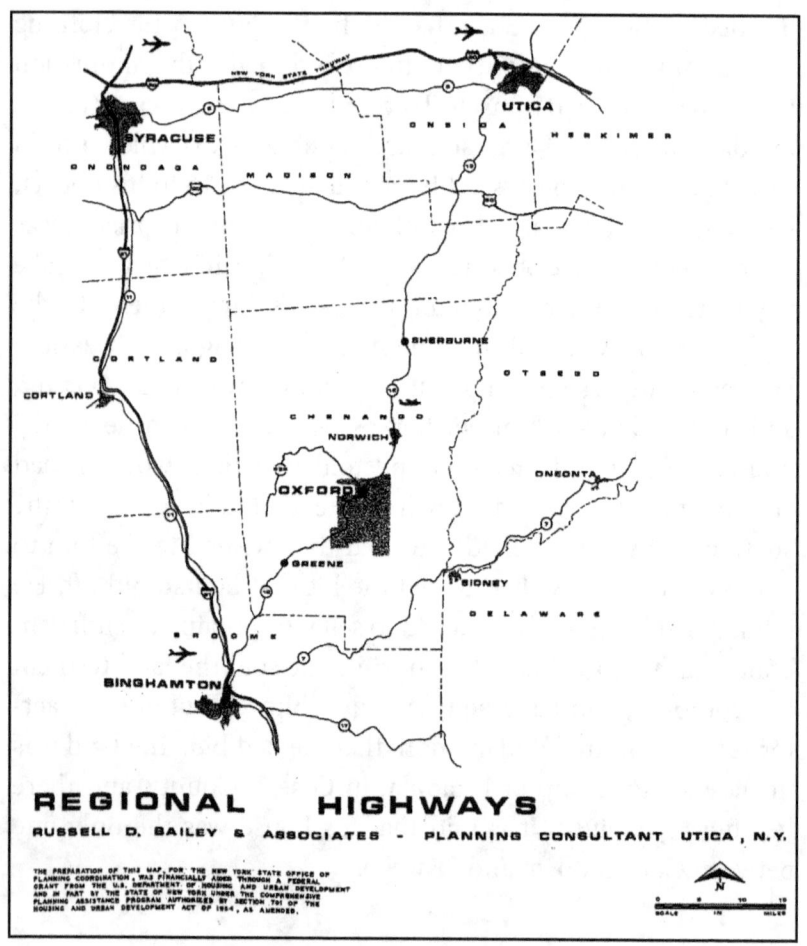

Present Day Township of Oxford

CHAPTER NINE
Hovey's Settlement
Beckoned by Low Prices

Even though Hovey immediately began using the name Oxford for the settlement, it was sometimes advertised as Hovey's Settlement. Settlers came mainly from New England where land prices for good farm land were high. News of the cheap land in central New York appeared in newspapers[62] and was also spread by word of mouth. Those attracted were often single men, with little more than an axe, a gun, some powder and a few dollars. Sometimes a family arrived with an ox cart and a few household possessions, as had Benjamin Hovey's. To house them, Benjamin had to see to it that the land was cleared of towering timber. This was done by a unique method. Wherever there was a row of trees, they would be undercut in the same direction. Then the first tree in the row would be felled so as to knock down all the trees in the row, just like toppling a line of dominoes standing on end, kaboom!

After lots were surveyed and sold, cabins had to be built. Before the first sawmill was established, this was accomplished by a "logging bee" in which the whole community joined. After the trees were felled and logs were cut to the right length and carefully notched, the bee commenced. As many as thirty men with yokes of oxen took part. Two of the logs with the largest diameter were placed in position to receive two more and thus the foundation laid. Then after being duly notched another tier was placed near the ends fitted together in the saddle cut in the lower tier. As walls grew higher, it took many hands to push the heavy green logs up to their proper notch.

The next day, before boards were available, elm bark peeled and dried in the sun was laid out on the roof timbers to keep out the rain. In good weather this took only two days. The owner was left to fill in the chinks between the logs with mud or clay. The hills surrounding the valley had abundant springs, providing sweet freshwater. About 1793, a sawmill was established on Hovey Creek west of the river. Thus later settlers had boards and beams to erect frame buildings.

As shown in the illustration by Rebecca Wilkinson on the next page Hovey laid out the town with spacious oval Washington Park on the east side and stately Lafayette Square (S) on the west side of the Chenango River. The first Oxford Academy (A) is shown just left of the top of the Washington Park oval and Hovey's first hut (H) at the top of Fort Hill.

The typical farm family owned two or three cows, a pig or two, a flock of chickens and sometimes ducks or geese. Barns were small, usually one-story affairs, about 30 by 40 feet with lean-tos on one side for the cows in winter. Hay was kept in the barn and during the summer, the cows were milked in the yard and kept in pasture. In late fall, the cows were bred so in the spring a new calf arrived. Sometimes an extra milk-fed calf was butchered early; the liver was so tender it could be cut with a spoon or fork if one had one.

During the summer, farmers made butter and kept it in firkins. In the fall they would sell the butter and settle any debts with the proceeds. Some farms had a hired man for six months

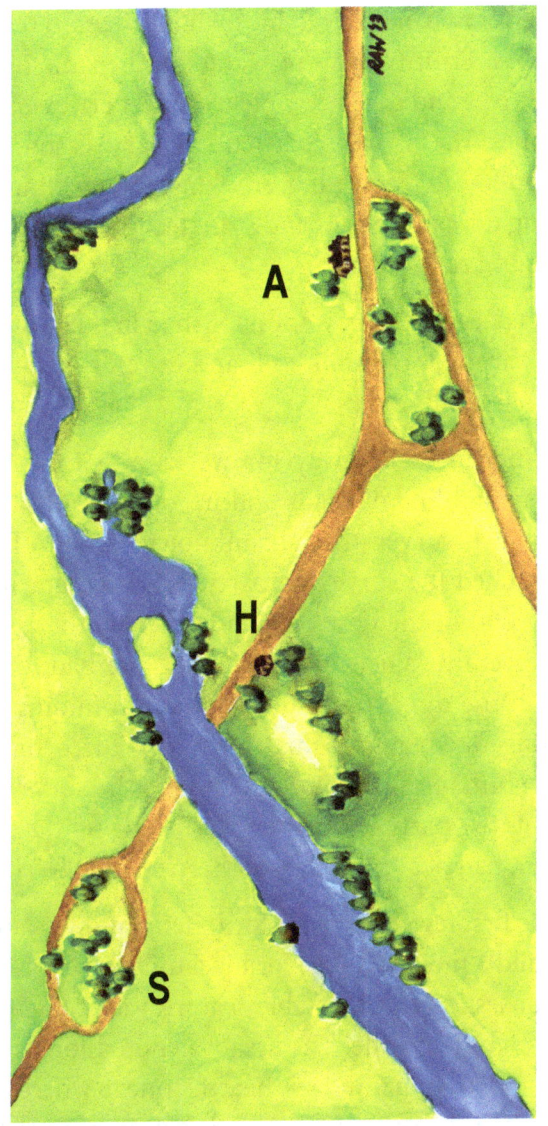

Hovey's Settlement illustration by Rebecca Wilkinson.

of the year. Every farmer raised his own meat, grain (chiefly rye) and vegetables. Fruit trees were planted to become orchards in the future. Wives and daughters picked wild berries and nuts for jams and jellies. The fall was a particularly busy season. There was butchering followed by corning, smoking and pickling. Potatoes had to be dug up, cabbage cut and stored, corn picked and stored in underground root cellars.

Shortly a cheese factory was established in the nearby hamlet of Preston. Farmers sold milk to it and in return received whey to feed to their cattle and pigs.

Benjamin had to be away for weeks at a time to survey, supervise the building of roads and negotiate land sales. It was during one such survey that an unknown Indian of powerful build approached the surveying party as it was returning to its cabin at the end of the day. He inquired if another Indian had passed by recently. When informed that one had, the warrior proceeded in the direction indicated, and on finding the other Indian sitting down buried his tomahawk three times in his skull, killing him instantly. On returning to the surveyors' cabin for the night, the party learned he was avenging the murder of his sister that had occurred in a southern state.

After the first few years in Oxford, Benjamin was able to hire help and build a modest house for his family. Like the early New England houses, its most notable feature was a huge fireplace, sometimes eight feet wide. The area was noted for its bluestone and oxen could drag an immense hearthstone to where it could be wedged in place. The cavernous opening was spanned by a large square lintel beam. Above and behind was a trammel bar from which pots and kettles were suspended. On the chimney above the fireplace was a mantel holding a host of utensils, including a candle mold, candlesticks, a sausage stuffer and a spice mill. In front of the fireplace was a settee with a high back so one could warm oneself by the fire without being chilled on the back by the draft of cold air being drawn to the cavernous chimney. By 1798, the Hovey house was virtually complete with rough wide-board floors of white pine.

In this house he opened Oxford's first store and conducted a land sales office. This he needed because, as mentioned above, he had purchased from Marinus Willett 4.449 out of the 7,049 acres in the Gore west of the Chenango River. The purchase price was 953 pounds, just a few pence more than the cost to Willett, who kept about 2,600 acres, including a number of choice river front lots.

In New York, townships are the smallest unit of state government. A number of towns form a county. Oxford was originally in the vast township of Fayette in Tioga County. Fayette was surveyed by the State's Surveyor General to contain 100 lots, each of 640 acres (a square mile). On January 19, 1793, the township was split in the middle into the towns of Oxford on the Chenango River and Guilford on the Unadilla. Benjamin Hovey was Oxford's first Superintendent. The first town meeting was held in April 1794, at his house.

The reasonable price of tillable land beckoned many families from crowded New England, including Theodore Burr, Aaron's cousin. He came to Oxford in 1793 when only 21 years old. The next year he built a grist mill, eliminating the need to grind grain with a mortar and pestle or the long canoe trip to the nearest mill. By 1800 he had built the first stringer bridge across the Chenango. He later became famous for inventing and patenting the Burr truss bridge, thousands of which were built all over America.

Jonathan Baldwin, a close friend of Theodore Burr, also came in 1793. He was noted for his skill at many occupations and for his ferocious temper. One sunny hot summer day he finished haying and stacked his hay beside the river. Suddenly a terrific rain storm came down the valley and, to his dismay, washed the stacks away. He ran to the river attempting to control his temper. With a mighty heave, he threw his pitchfork into it, crying out "If God Almighty wants that hay, then He wants a fork to pitch it with."[63]

Today, like so many other small towns and villages in New York State, no longer the center of a farming community, no longer served by railroad or canal, no longer attracting the shoppers now gone to the Walmart out of town, Oxford has recently developed a new comprehensive Town and Village Plan.

This Plan states that Oxford is a thriving community of engaged and caring residents who support creative local initiatives toward economic self-sufficiency. Oxford welcomes new residents, businesses and visitors to share its rural character and small town quality of life and stewardship of its rich historic and natural resources.

CHAPTER TEN
Founding the Oxford Academy
No Yankee without the means of education

Benjamin Hovey felt education was very important. The story of the apprehension of the British spy, Major Andre, by three highwaymen who stole his boots, showed how even a little education could change the course of the War. Finding papers in the boots, John Paulding, the only ruffian who could read, exclaimed "This is a spy!" and the kidnapping of George Washington by Benedict Arnold was thus adverted.[64] So Hovey, soon after establishing Oxford, set about establishing the Oxford Academy. Its Charter dated January 12, 1793, recites that the subscribers have erected an Academy and asks that the Regents incorporate it with Benjamin Hovey, Uri Tracy and 16 other named trustees. The Charter was granted by the Regents on January 24, 1794. It was one of the first four school charters granted by the state west of the Hudson River.

The Academy was housed in the first frame building erected in Oxford. It was built in the autumn of 1792 at the northwest end of Washington Park. This beautiful park laid out at the founding of Oxford still exists. Its spacious oval reminds one of some of the most graceful of New England villages. The cost of materials to build the first Academy was advanced by Hovey. At a meeting in April 1794, the Academy's Board of Trustees voted to reimburse him in the amount of 164 pounds, 13 shilling and 6 pence. In the autumn of 1799 the second building was erected but was destroyed by fire before it was ever used. The Academy was reopened in 1806 in the third Academy building.

Benjamin was President of the Board of Trustees for as long as he remained in Oxford, ten years. His son-in-law, Uri Tracy, was the first teacher and principal. From its outset, the Academy set high standards. Uri Tracy decreed "No Scholar is to be admitted into the School until he can spell well, and read the lessons in Mr. Webster's first part, and begin to read in Webster's third part." To meet his requirements the wife of one of the early settlers gave lessons in her home.

On the first and second of August in 1854, the Academy celebrated the sixtieth year of its founding with a Jubilee. Henry R. Mygatt, President of the Board of Trustees, gave the welcoming address, as follows:

"The merry peels of the Church bells, and the sound of music, have gathered here after a sultry day refreshed in the mellow and beautiful light of sunset. It is the eve of the Jubilee. Sixty years ago, this town was incorporated by the Legislature of the State. And at an early day, in 1794, this Academy was chartered by the Regents of the University. Thirty years thereafter it was my good fortune to be a student here, and after the hand of Time has moved forward thirty years more, as the representative of the Board of Trustees, and of the Home Committee of former students, as well as on behalf of my fellow citizens, I cordially welcome you, teachers, students, friends, to the dedication of a new edifice for the increase and diffusion of knowledge among men. Although the fifth academic building is to be dedicated here, that those who search after knowledge and truth may be satisfied, it is the first time that the dispersed of all climates, ages, professions and pursuits, have returned to the place where in their youth they had imbibed instruction and contracted friendships as lasting as life. Sixty years ago, the strife of the Revolution had just ceased, and religious and civil freedom had been unchained. But little more than sixty years ago the Oneida canton of the Iroquois nation roamed over the dense and unbroken forests along the banks of the beautiful Chenango, fearless, unmolested and free. The educated and practical man, the Puritan from New England, came and hastily built his log house; and with a wisdom unprecedented in the annals of time, the first framed building that he built here was the Academy. Education spread its mantle of light over the land, and art, science and literature began to bud to its full fruition. Uri Tracy, a graduate of Yale College, a minister of the Gospel, was the first principal of the Academy. To the savage the school had sprung up like an enchantment, but to the contemplative mind of the dependent settler it revealed the smile of a kind Providence, who was illuminating the moral darkness of the valley by religion and learning."

One may fault Mr. Mygatt for implying that Benjamin Hovey was educated rather than uneducated and a Puritan rather than a Universalist, but one can find no fault with his loquaciousness, his mastery of coordinate, subordinate and mixed-pattern sentences! The next day of the Jubilee, W. H. Hyde gave an address no less nostalgic, as follows:

"The shades of evening are gathering; what a sea of gorgeousness on the autumn forest! We hear the lightly dip of paddles in the river and a canoe darts towards the landing on the shore. What strange beings are these? They seem regardless of the ruin that is gradually gathering over the race. Can it be that they do not see the oncoming destruction that awaits them, while they see the little academy on the Common, the occasional dwelling, and hear the woodman's axe, whose strokes for them:

Like muffled drums are beating funeral marches to the grave? That tall man with whom they are talking, bartering at the log house, is Benjamin Hovey, the senior trustee of the Academy. Few men have passed a more eventful life. Having seen the fruition of his labors, and the harvest of his early toil and suffering, in the flourishing village around him, rapidly increasing in population and wealth, he looked for new projects with an ambition fed by his own innate energy and a spirit of enterprise faltering at no point beyond which were seen new fields open for its gratification."

From its founding to 1793, the Oxford Academy was considered to be one of the leading private boarding and day schools in western New York. As the blue stone quarries near Oxford felt increasing competition from cement and the hoe and other businesses in Oxford were replaced by manufacturers in the mid-west and south, the means to continue as a private school decreased and in 1893 the Academy affiliated with the state's public school system. It now thrives as the Oxford Academy and Central Schools with two campuses dedicated today to the education of almost 1,000 students.

As mentioned by Mr. Mygatt, Uri Tracy graduated from Yale in 1789, and was ordained as a Presbyterian minister. He came to Oxford shortly after it was founded as a missionary to the Native Americans. Apparently his mission was a success for there are no reports of disputes with them. He courted and on August 28, 1793, married Benjamin and Lydia's eldest daughter, Ruth, four months before her 18th birthday. He became a teacher and principal of the Oxford Academy and served in that capacity for many years.

Unlike his father, Benjamin's eldest son, Alfred, did have an education. He attended the Academy briefly in its early years. Benjamin's grandson, Franklin Colvin Hovey, was a boarder at the Academy, where he developed a great love for the tragedies of Shakespeare and the adventure stories of James Fennimore Cooper, before graduating in 1798, to head west with the 1849 gold rush to California.

To do justice to his duties as Trustee of the Academy, Supervisor of the Township, land agent, store keeper, pound master and other jobs from time to time, Benjamin needed help. He found it in a young man named James Glover. Glover appears to have handled his correspondence and served as the right-hand man so long as Benjamin remained in Oxford. In all probability he arrived in Oxford with nothing more than an axe and gun, but he brought with him something that Benjamin did not have, an education and the ability to write. When one compares the road contract written by Benjamin before James Glover arrived on the scene and the letter to General Morris and Memorial to Congress written after that event, it is evident Benjamin had a skilled assistant.

James Glover, who became a part of the family in 1795 when he married the second Hovey daughter, Alphena. His portrait shown at right is attributed to Otis Hovey, who was born after the family moved to Oxford, New York. Like many families sired by athletic, vigorous, business-oriented parents, one or more of the sons or

Alphena Hovey Glover

The portraits of James and Alphena Hovey Glover are reproduced courtesy of Rick and Russell Hauptman, descendants of James and Alphena Hovey Glover.

daughters turns his or her back on the life of toil, getting and spending and turns to art, as did Otis, who moved to New York City to pursue a career as a portrait painter. The portrait of Alphena Hovey Glover, above is also attributed to Otis.

CHAPTER ELEVEN
Founding Chenango County
Friendship with a Burr has prickles

Soon after Benjamin Hovey arrived in Oxford he found it necessary to petition the Assembly to straighten out the boundaries of Montgomery County.

In 1795, Benjamin's term as Supervisor of the town of Oxford ended and he did not seek that office again. Instead the next year, 1796, Benjamin ran for the Tioga County seat in the New York Assembly against Caleb Hyde, a Revolutionary War veteran who had fought in the battle of Saratoga. Hyde claimed he had the most votes, but these included the votes reported by a certain town whose inspectors had not signed the report as required by law. If the votes of that town had not been counted, Hovey would have won. Hovey hired a lawyer to press his case but after a committee report and debate, the Assembly ignored the irregularity and resolved that Hyde was the duly elected Assemblyman from Tioga County, 82 to 11. Aaron Burr, who had been elected to the Assembly after completing his term in the United States Senate, voted for Hyde.

Notwithstanding this defeat, Hovey ran again as a Democratic-Republican (States-Rights) candidate for the legislature. He had learned that he had to lighten up his appeal as a candidate who would bring a new county to his constituents with humor. In those days ethnic jokes were politically correct and frequently told. He doubtless had several about the Praying Nipmugs in Oxford, Massachusetts, even their name was funny! Also barnyard humor was needed. Having the rival politician stand on a mound in the barnyard to announce his platform and then observe he was standing on a platform of manure brought a laugh. He likely also entertained a lot. This led to his election in 1798. Set forth below is the only known sketch of this Assemblyman in the New York legislature:

Benjamin's resolute jaw and facial features also appear in photographs of his eldest son, Alfred.

Benjamin Hovey introduced several petitions from the eastern part of Tioga County praying for its division. These were referred to a committee on which he was a member. On January 29, 1798, the committee obtained leave to bring in a bill entitled "An Act to excerpt part of the Counties of Tioga and Herkimer into a separate County." This Act was adopted on March 15, 1798, and so Chenango County was created.

MAP OF CHENANGO COUNTY
MARCH 15, 1798

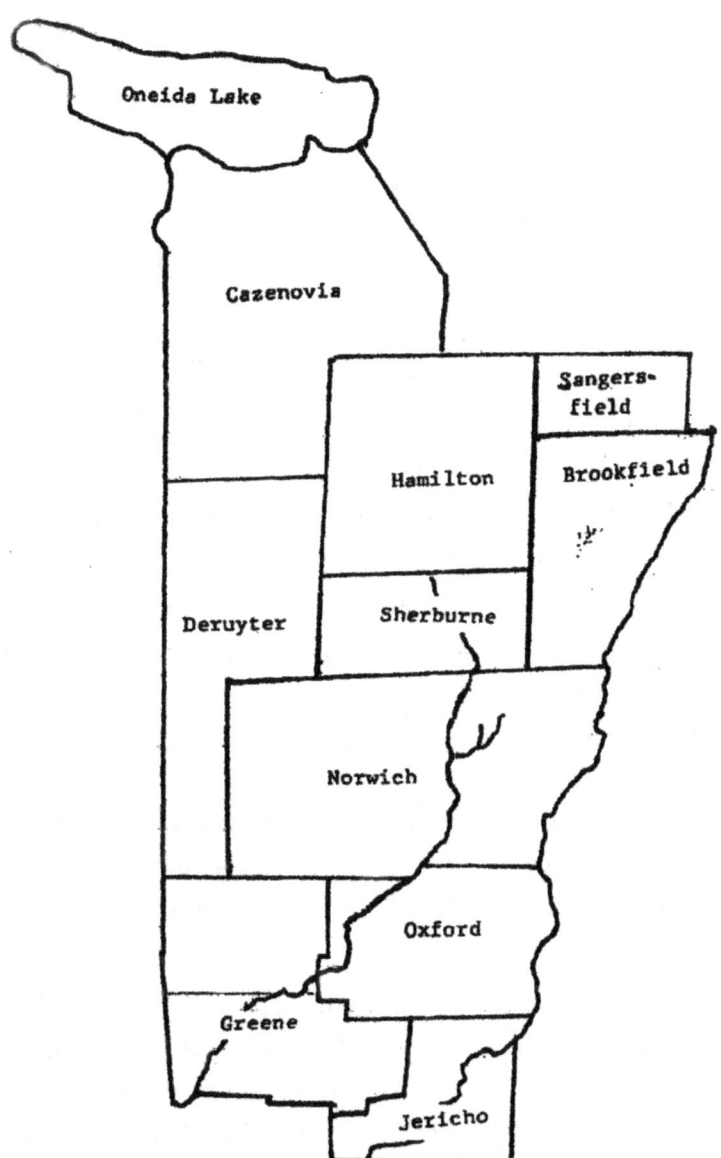

As shown on the map shown on the next page, Chenango County was originally bounded on the east by the Unadilla River and ran all the way north to Lake Oneida.[65] It lies west of the Catskill Mountains and Susquehanna River in Central New York. Its surface is generally hilly. Most of these hills run north and south with broad summits trimmed eons ago by the retreating glaciers to a uniform height, making them ideal for growing fruit trees and staples as well as for grazing farm animals. Early settlers had to clear the standing timber. There was an over abundance for the sawmill soon set up. The excess timber was burned to ashes to make lye and soap.

A separate county brought many opportunities for Oxford and the Hovey family. For Benjamin's son-in-law, Uri Tracy, a minister and Academy principal, it provided several additional positions: Chenango County Sheriff from 1798 to 1801, County Clerk from 1801 to 1815, postmaster from 1802 to 1805, election to the United States Congress three times and appointment as County Judge from 1819 to 1823.

Two other sons-in-law also benefited. Zalmon Smith married the Hoveys' third daughter, Nancy, and with her ran a tavern. He also served as Superintendent of Highways. Nathaniel Locke, the surveyor, married Hovey's fourth daughter, Mary. He succeeded Uri Tracy as Sheriff of Chenango County in 1801, as soon as Uri Tracy became the County Clerk. Nathaniel and Mary were the parents of C. F. T. Locke, who for many years was Oxford's leading storekeeper.

In addition to the advantages stemming from the creation of Chenango County, in the assembly Benjamin met many leaders of the state, including Aaron Burr whose early life and education have been described in Chapter One. Burr, in his quest for their support as potential members of the Electoral College, went out of his way to become a friend and mentor for Benjamin

Aaron Burr

Hovey and other Assemblymen. Burr later went on to court the legislators in New England and Virginia.

On first meeting Burr has been described as "a man of an erect and dignified deportment—his presence is commanding—his aspect mild, firm, luminous and impressive. ... The eyebrows are thin, nearly horizontal, and too far from the eye; his nose rather inclined to the right side; gently elevated which conveys a degree of haughtiness; too obtuse at the end for a great acuteness of penetration, brilliancy of wit or poignancy of satire, and too small to sustain his capacious and ample forehead. His eyes are ... of a dark hazel, and, from the shade of his projecting eye bones and brows, appear black; they glow ... and scintillate with the most tremulous and tearful sensibility—they roll with the celerity and phrensy of poetic fervour, and beam with the most vivid and piercing rays of genius. His mouth is large; his voice is clear, manly and melodious; his lips are thin, extremely flexible, and when silent, gently closed ... his chin is rather retreating and voluptuous. ..."[66]

It was such a charismatic figure that Benjamin met. They immediately had much in common. They were within a year of being the same age. Both had fought in the Revolutionary War; Burr with particular distinction in the attack on Quebec, had risen to the rank of Lieutenant Colonel in the Continental Army, before retiring due to ill health. Hovey had served in the militia on four occasions (including Shay's rebellion) and was now a Lieutenant Colonel commanding a Regiment. Both had a wide circle of friends, including such mutual friends as General Marinus Willett and Burr's cousin, Theodore, whom they liked to entertain. Both were interested in land developments in western New York. Their major difference was in education. Hovey had little; Burr was well educated. He had first served as Assemblyman in 1784 and 1785. Then, after such prestigious positions as New

York Attorney General and United States Senator, returned to the Assembly for two more terms ending in 1800. Burr looked at the less prestigious position of an Assemblyman as a stepping stone from which to vault to much higher office. The State Legislatures were the key to the office of President and Vice President for they elected the members of the Electoral College.[67]

Notwithstanding his success as a solder, lawyer and politician, Burr was frequently in debt, engaging in land speculation and a most extravagant life style. As a widower, Burr had a great interest in the education of young Theodosia and their social status, enhanced by acquiring in 1793 the magnificent estate named Richmond Hill previously described. In three different accounts of his life Benjamin Hovey is likewise chided for entertaining a large circle of friends, more than his purse could bear. One wonders whether he caught this trait at Richmond Hill on a visit to see Burr. Of course, Hovey was not so profligate to entertain on the scale of Burr. In rural and rustic Oxford tender morsels of pork sliced from a fat pig turned on a spit over an open fire for at least 24 hours, accompanied by roasted ears of corn, washed down with hard cider and followed by apple and peach pies would be more suitable entertainment. In all likelihood such events preceded both his unsuccessful run for the Assembly in 1796 and successful election in 1798.

During their final year as Assemblymen, 1799, Burr introduced a bill for supplying the City of New York "with pure and wholesome water." What Alexander Hamilton and the Federalists did not realize was that the charter of the Manhattan Company also authorized a bank; hence the Bank of the Manhattan Company came into existence. This broke the stranglehold the Federalists had on banking, through the only two banks in New York, a branch of the Bank of the United States and Mr. Hamilton's Bank of New York.

The presidential election of 1800 pitted John Adams, the incumbent Federalist President against Thomas Jefferson the Democratic Republican (States-Rights) candidate. To balance the Virginian, Jefferson, a northerner was needed and it came down to either George Clinton or Aaron Burr. With the help of the Burrites from New York City, Burr became Jefferson's running mate. Burr's bitterest opponent was the Federalist, Alexander Hamilton. Hamilton perhaps best pictured and summarized the distrust of Burr by his detractors when he wrote to James Bayard on January 16, 1801, as follows:

"As to Burr these things are admitted and cannot be denied, that he is a man of extreme and irregular ambition — that he is selfish to a degree which excludes all social affections & that he is decidedly profligate. ... But it is said 1st that he is artful and dexterous to accomplish his ends ... ." Hamilton later says: "If Burr's conversation can be credited he is not very far from being a visionary. ... The truth is that Burr is a man of very subtle imagination, and a mind of this make is rarely free from ingenious whimsies. ... I think that it is almost certain that he will try usurpation. And the attempt will involve great mischief."

Hovey could not have expected that his new-found friend would not only leap from the New York Assembly to be the Vice Presidential candidate but would also wind up with 73 electoral votes, the same as Thomas Jefferson's for President. Prior to the ratification of its 12th Amendment in 1812, the Constitution provided that electors cast two votes without distinguishing between President and Vice President. If a tie occurred, the House of Representatives should immediately choose who was to be President. The Federalists, seeing that John Adams, their candidate, was out of the running, supported Burr, as the lesser of two evils, rather than the arch Republican, Thomas Jefferson. Burr had written to Samuel Smith on December 16, 1800, that he would step out of the way in case of a tie. "It is highly unlikely that I shall have an equal number of votes with Mr. Jefferson, but if such should be the result, every man that knows me ought to know that I should utterly disclaim all competition—Be assured that the federal party can entertain no wish for such an exchange. As to my friends—they would dishonor my views and insult my feelings by harboring a suspicion that I could submit to being instrumental in counteracting the wishes and expectations of the U.S." When the tie actually occurred, however, Burr remained silent. He did nothing to break the deadlock for thirty-six tie ballots from the 11th to the 17th of February, 1801. The tie was finally broken when a Federalist from Delaware withdrew his vote for Burr. This Federalist was the same James Bayard to whom Hamilton had written disparagingly of Burr. He allegedly received a message from an emissary of Jefferson that Jefferson would meet his demand for a strong Navy and the appointment of James Latimer as Collector of Customs for the Port of Philadelphia. After he withdrew his vote for Burr, others followed and Jefferson was elected as the third President. Jefferson later denied that he had authorized any emissary to make this deal, stating no "Republican ever uttered the most distant hint to me about submitting to any conditions or giving assurances to anybody."[68]

Thomas Jefferson

CHAPTER TWELVE

Convicted by Court Martial

Crushed in Spirit?

Following the end of the Revolutionary War, there was much opposition to a standing army. It was considered the crushing fist of tyranny. The British had imposed such an army on the Massachusetts Bay Colony and housed soldiers in the home of the residents of Boston. To address such tyranny, the Bill of Rights added ten amendments to the Constitution. The second of them states: "A well regulated militia being necessary for the security of a free state, the right of the people to keep and bear arms shall not be infringed." The third prohibits quartering troops in homes except in time of war.

Furthermore, in New York there were still occasionally Indian raids. Accordingly, a Regiment of Militia at Oxford under the command of Lieutenant Colonel Benjamin Hovey had been established in 1793. In fact the only letter from Benjamin Hovey known to exist was sent to General Jacob Morris, a Revolutionary War soldier and Godson of George Washington, who headed a Division of the Militia.[69] It reads:

"Oxford, May 28th, 1799

Dear Sir

The Adgt. Gen'l will be at Oxford on Saturday, 8th of June, at which time I hope to be honored with your company. On Friday morning the Reverend Mr. Camp will address himself to the militia, in the afternoon you and the Gen'l can go on to the Butternuts, and on Monday morning be at Otego. Pleas (sic) to give Maj'r Edwards an invitation and be so kind as to inform me by Next Post.

I am with esteem your Humble servt.

BENJ. HOVEY

GEN'L MORRIS"

On April 1, 1801, John Jay, the Federalist lame duck Governor of New York, ordered the militia of the State to hold a parade on Monday, June 8th of that year. The order was transmitted to each Brigade. The Brigadier General commanding Hovey's Regiment was Jonathan Forman. The Brigade headquarters was at Cazenovia in what was then Chenango but is now Madison County about 60 miles northwest of Oxford. Forman had served in the State Assembly at the same time as Hovey and was a staunch Federalist. He may well have been displeased with the way Hovey split off parts of Tioga and Herkimer Counties to create Chenango so as to include Cazenovia. It is possible also that Forman had a grudge against Hovey, who had been granted 5,000 acres in the "Road Township" as payment for completing a "two ox cart" road.

On receipt of the Governor's order, Forman wrote a letter for delivery to Lieutenant Colonel Benjamin Hovey. This letter enclosed an Order by the Brigade, dated April 19, 1801, to hold the parade and was entrusted to a Major Ray for delivery by hand. Major Ray did not deliver the letter to Hovey. Instead he delivered it to his right hand man, James Glover, who had married Hovey's second daughter, Alphena. Hovey failed to call out his Regiment for a parade on Monday, June 8, 1801.

Hovey, charged with violating the Governor's Order of April 1 and disobeying the Brigade Order of April 20, was subjected to a trial by Court Martial. At the trial Ray testified that he saw Hovey hold the letter in his hand and say either he would not obey it or that he would not pay any attention to it. The Court Martial convicted Hovey of violating the order of April 1 and the Brigade Order of April 20 and stripped him of his rank.

According to the *Annals of Oxford*, the Court Martial was a Federal Court Martial and Hovey was crushed in spirit. It is obvious it was not a Federal Court Martial. The fact of the matter is that Brigadier General Jonathan Forman, who was the main instigator of the charges, had served with some distinction in the Continental Army under Washington and he and others involved may have used Continental Army procedures rather than those of the New York Militia. Forman was originally from New Jersey, but like Hovey had been bitten by the land speculation bug, in his case moving to Cazenovia, New York, about 60 miles northwest of Oxford. What the reporters of a Federal Court Martial should have said is that it was a Court Martial instigated by a member of the Federalist Party.

Far from being crushed in spirit, Hovey made a timely appeal. George Clinton, who had succeeded John Jay as Governor of New York on July 1, 1801, and thus became Commander in Chief of the Militia, heard the appeal. The decision on appeal is set forth in full in a General Order dated December 16, 1801. In it, Clinton first observed it was his duty to enforce due obedience from subordinate officers to their superiors. Then in a dazzling display of his early legal training, he cut through the Court Martial proceedings as quickly as Benjamin's keen axe notched logs for his first cabin. His opinion would do credit to such leading lawyers of that day as John Adams, Aaron Burr or Henry Clay.

He detailed the irregularities to prevent their repetition and admonished officers to carefully examine the proceedings before pronouncing their determination of them. The first irregularity, instead of setting forth the questions and answers of the witnesses, only a summary was given. Second, the witness did not state to whom General Forman's letter was addressed or when it was delivered. Third, although the witness saw the letter in the hands of Hovey, he did not know if the Order itself came into his hands. Fourth, although the witness stated he heard Hovey say he should not obey the Orders or he would not pay attention to them, he did not state at what time or under what circumstances this happened or to what Orders Hovey alluded. Fifth, a letter dated May 19, 1801, from Hovey to the witness, was presented without any proof that it was admitted into evidence.

So much for the substance. Clinton then exploded the procedures like a string of fire crackers lit by a sparkler on the Fourth of July. Forman's Brigade Order of April 19, directing Hovey to parade his Regiment on June 8 omitted the Commander in Chief's Orders but only made a general reference thereto without particularizing their import. Moreover, Hovey's letter to the witness was only a copy, not the original.

Continuing his fiery attack on the faulty procedures used to convict Hovey, Clinton points out that the Order for a trial preceded service of a notice of the charges against Hovey and his arrest. Adding insult to injury, the charges on which he was tried were different from the charges tardily served on him. He was tried for failing to obey a Brigade Order of April 20 whereas the actual Order was dated April 19.

Before the trial Hovey had applied for an adjournment. He pointed out that he had only six days to prepare for the trial and his witnesses lived in different counties and the abode of the President of the Court Martial was sixty miles distant. The Court Martial overruled his application on two grounds, first it was unprecedented and second, even if it had been granted, Hovey could not exculpate himself.

Clinton then summarized the Act governing the militia and stated that he was decidedly of the opinion that the issuing of an Order for convening a Court Martial to try an officer for an arrest before the arrest is actually made and a copy of the charges served on him was illegal and improper. It was also illegal and improper to try an officer on charges varying from those served on him. He found a general charge of disobedience without stating the point of duty on which the charge is founded is contrary to law.

He found that the reason for refusing an adjournment was repugnant to justice, incorrect and untenable. (How can you say that witnesses who have not been allowed to testify could not exculpate the defendant?) Finally, Clinton found there was no evidence of disobedience of any Order of the Commander-in-Chief or of the Brigade Order of April 20. Even if the Brigade Order of April 19 was intended, it does not appear that it came into the hands of Hovey.

Further there was no proof he neglected his duty or disobeyed any Orders. Accordingly, Clinton disaffirmed the judgment of the Court Martial and Hovey was returned to rank.[70]

At this time, as set forth in the Federalist Papers, a standing army was considered a threat to liberty and the state militias controlled by the governors of the several states symbolized their independent sovereignty, except when called up for federal service when the President becomes their commander in chief.[71]

Benjamin Hovey was promoted to Brigadier General of the Fifth Division of Militia, the Chenango County Brigade, in January 1802 at the first meeting of the Council on Appointments after the decision on appeal. At the same meeting Brigadier General Jonathan Forman was cashiered.

CHAPTER THIRTEEN
Promoted to General
Buttermilk and Brandy

The decision to promote Benjamin Hovey to Brigadier General and strip Jonathan Forman of that rank raised a storm of protest in Forman's former Regiment of militia based in Cazenovia. Many of the militiamen were Federalists appointed by John Jay, who had been the Governor for the preceding six years. Thirty-odd officers tendered their resignations. The matter became a cause célèbre in the press of that day. It reported their polemic in detail, starting with the statement "That the reinstating of Benjamin Hovey as Lieutenant Colonel and the removal of Brigadier General Jonathan Forman, Esq. has excited in their breasts the most lively emotions of indignation and regret" and ending with, "when they are told of the importance of a well regulated militia, and that too much attention can hardly be devoted to that estimable object; while military discipline is trampled upon, and subordination has become the foot ball of derision; that then it is high time that those who are not totally lost to all sense of dignity, to resign commissions which they cannot hold any longer with honor to themselves or usefulness to the community."[72, 73]

Notwithstanding, the ruling of George Clinton, as Commander in Chief of the Militia, Major General Myers ordered a further Court Martial of Lieutenant Colonel Hovey. This time he was duly arrested and trial was noticed in the Court House in Cooperstown. Major General Myers expended every effort to correct the technical errors found by Clinton in the first trial. The Court met on May 27, 1802, and found that the fact that Hovey was now a Brigadier General "must supersede all the authority of the Court appointed to try him as Lieutenant Colonel, and that all the proceedings against him under the arrest aforesaid shall cease and abate."[74]

The Cazenovia Militia was still not ready to let the matter drop. Two of them, Captain Lemuel Kingsbury and Lieutenant Ebenezer Lyon assigned as their reason an animadvert (an obsolete word for polite disapproval) of the decision of the Governor in disaffirming the conviction of Hovey by the Court Martial. They then went on to censure and condemn the Council on the removal of Forman. The Council found this reprehensible and removed all the dissidents from their office save for seven who apologized to the Governor for their criticism.

This disciplinary action brought, like some laws in physics, an equal and opposite reaction. General Training or Militia days, except in war time, were detested by most able-bodied men. Farmers, particularly in planting and growing seasons, called them "malicious" days. Dr. Timothy Dwight, President of Yale, visited Cazenovia in the Chenango Valley in September 1804. He told of reviewing the militia, saying: "The officers lately commanding the regiment were men of worth and reputation. They also possessed a considerable share of military skill, spirit and ambition. Under their discipline the regiment had become distinguished for peculiar improvements in every part of military character. When those officers were disposed by the government of the State, all non-commissioned officers of the regiment resigned, but their resignations were not accepted." He went on to explain that the new political appointees had no military knowledge or training. The militia pretended that they did not know even the simplest command.[75] The men asked to be shown. The officers pleaded with them and then swore at them. The State finally restored the veteran officers but allowed the political appointees to retain their commissions.

Thus, Benjamin Hovey's career as a Brigadier General was launched in a storm of political controversy and lasted only two years, from 1802 until March 9, 1804, when he resigned in order to devote all his energies to the Ohio Canal project. Nevertheless, there are many stories that refer to him as General Hovey both before and after he held that rank. This shows the high esteem in which he was held by all who knew him, excepting Jonathan Forman and the Cazenovia Militia. One of the most amusing of these stories appears in the *Annals of Oxford, New York,* and is set forth below:

Josiah Hackett

Yankee Doodle, twist the cat
Buttermilk and Brandy
Guess I'll bet my Sunday Hat
They'll find I'm a Boy quite handy.

Thus sang Josiah Hackett as he entered the village on the 19th day of July, 1798, a beautiful summer afternoon with a touch of rain in the wind. He was a man of forty years, dressed in short breeches, long stockings with accompanying shoe buckles, and carried a musket over his shoulder, which he termed 'the Bloodsucker.' Approaching a humble abode, whose friendly door stood open and from which the housewife looked forth, he addressed her as follows:

"Madame, I'm a shoemaker, a soldier, and a traveler, seeking a place of shelter until I can make arrangements to locate in this section of God's country. I've been at the Inn, but figs and catnip! Their rooms are taken for the night, and the landlord couldn't lodge another person nohow. Can you lodge me till morning?"

"Yes" was the smiling reply. "I think we may make room for you, though my husband, Mr. Hovey, is not at home at present. He is at the Academy, where Justice Kent, Esq. is holding court. But you look tired, come in and wait. He will be home soon."

"Thank ye, ma'am. I am that tired that if I was carried to the highest court of juncture I couldn't make a move to resist."

He was ushered into the kitchen, whose floor of rough boards was cleanly swept and the huge stone fireplace was apparently ready for the preparation of the evening meal. On the mantel over the fireplace stood a candlestick, a sausage stuffer, a spice mill and a candle mold. By the side of the fireplace stood a smoke-blackened almanac, and by the hearth stood a high-backed settle, a sheltered seat for the long winter evenings. Within a short time Gen. Hovey appeared and soon the two were busily engaged in conversation. In answer to a question about himself Josiah replied:

"I am from Lyme, Conn., where I was born in 1758. When the alarm that preceded the Battle of Bunker Hill spread throughout the country, I took my musket, which I call 'The Bloodsucker,' and started for the scene of the conflict, where we were busier than a bee at a pumpkin blow. Since then my musket goes where I go. She's a quick witted jade, but trusty and true."

"What is your business here?" asked Gen. Hovey.

"I am a shoemaker and want to locate in this new country, and was told you are a land agent. I made inquiries at the Inn for lodgings, but could not get in. 'Rabbit ye, an' be darned', says I, and moved along." "No, they have more than they can accommodate," replied General Hovey, "Hon. James Kent, Esq., one of the Justices of the Supreme Court of judicature in this State, held Circuit Court here today, the first in the history of this youthful County."

"Oh, by the lorry and living jingo! Had I known that court was in session I might have come earlier, as I would have liked to heard the proceedings," said Josiah as he took a pipe and tobacco from his pocket.

"They were not interesting as there was no business to come before the court at this sitting. It was a mere matter of form you know. But Mr. Justice Kent is a keen man, and I predict he will be at least the Chancellor some day."

"Oh, well, I haven't lost a nation sight of jigger-marees, if there was no business to come before the court."

"No," replied the General, "but as to your business here. You are a shoemaker, you say, and we need here a man of that trade as much as any other. The community is growing, and you'll get a good living."

"Figs and catnip! I'm not only a shoemaker but a patriot also, as 'The Bloodsucker' my trusty musket which has never misfired can testify. I came to this country to earn a living for myself, wife and little one, and I'll be soused in a butter tub if I don't do it. I also came for game, and those who know me best say I'm a good marksman. Uts, bobs, and butakins, but that won't do for me to say."

"Are you a patriot?"

"Yes. I saw a wonderation of fighting, but more about that some other time. Last fall my health was so poor that I thought I would have to lie down in the graveyard and draw the green coverlet over my poor old body for the long sleep. I couldn't set in meeting or scarcely lie in bed. A doctor told me I was conflicted with a complaint of the lungs, and I had better move out west when summer came, or my flesh would waste and I would become weaker and bowed down, 'All right,' says I, 'I insign to see what your advice is good for if it costs me my fireball colt!"[76]

"You appear quite rugged now."

"Yes, I have been on the way for several weeks and have got rid of flamation wheezing and difficulty in breathing. Ods, bodkins, but I like this new country, and we will locate here or a few miles out. 'Drather be out of the hamlet, where feel all over goose pimples, and where I'll have a better chance at game that abounds in this section. When 'The 'Bloodsucker' gets a fair chance at it, it will find the gizzard ripped out as quick as a pig can crack a walnut."

"Well I can locate you anywhere you choose. Let me see, what did I understand your name is ___?"

"Josiah Hackett, Si for short. A soldier, shoemaker and now a traveler. I love my country, and rabbit ye the day of its birth, the glorious Fourth, whose anniversary was just last week, is the day of the day for me. It is my solemn wish, and may the great and living Father grant it, that the hour that ends may come on the Fourth of July."

It was now the supper hour, and Mrs. Hovey called them in from the rear of the dwelling where they had been sitting. On the following morning, arrangements were made by which Josiah located near the 'Desserts' in the south part of the town, and it was he who gave the name to that section.

On July 4th, 1845, forty-seven years later, Luman Fish entered C.F.T. Locke's store and said:

Well Locke, "Uncle Si's got his wish at last."

"Do you mean old Si Hackett?" inquired Mr. Locke, as he proceeded to tie a pound of tea he had been weighing.

"Yes, he has always wanted to die on the Fourth of July, and today the end came. We'll never see old Si with 'The Bloodsucker' over his shoulder again."

"Well, well," said Mr. Locke, as he stepped in front of the counter. "We'll miss him and his musket. He was always firing a salute on Independence Day."

"Yes," was the reply, "and a better marksman I never saw. He came here when the town was new and there was plenty of game.

He used to say his musket was a quick-witted jade. But trusty and true."

"That's so," replied Locke. "He was a great hunter, and they say he fought bravely in the Revolution."

"Yes and he was that patriotic that to this day he could hardly bear to talk to an Englishman. And another thing, we'll miss him singing Yankee Doodle on all occasions."

"Well, if St. Peter hears him singing as he approaches, he'll be so astonished that Si will dodge in the gates of heaven without the countersign."

CHAPTER FOURTEEN

Founding the Canal Company

*The Ohio, bosom smooth,
a single instance only excepted.*

By the end of his two-year term in the Assembly, Benjamin Hovey may well have taken stock of his life. After sharing in the creation of a new life, he had not shirked his responsibility. He had adequately provided for that life, his wife and family, as witnessed by all four of his daughters, who were already successfully married. He had helped found a religion of universal forgiveness, forged a road to a new country, created a village, chartered an academy, established a county and met many leaders of his day. Given all that, he was still just a big fish in a small pond. Feeling his gills needed more oxygen, he set out to become a big fish in a big river.

There was considerable talk of separating New England, New York and New Jersey from the rest of the states. There was even more talk of expansion west to the Ohio River. James Wilkinson, a friend of Aaron Burr, had navigated the Ohio to the Mississippi and down it to New Orleans and back. James Monroe was negotiating the purchase of the Louisiana Territory from Napoleon. Among many opportunities provided by the opening of the west, Hovey's attention was drawn to the Ohio River and the prospect of great profits from improving its usefulness as a primary artery to western America by excavating a canal around its falls.

The Ohio River is formed where the Allegheny and Monongahela Rivers meet in what is now downtown Pittsburgh, Pennsylvania. It flows generally in a southwest by west direction some 981 miles to meet the Mississippi at Cairo, Illinois. In his only book, *Notes on the State of Virginia*, published in 1781/2, Thomas Jefferson stated: "The Ohio is the most beautiful river on earth. Its current gentle, waters clear and bosom smooth and unbroken by rocks and rapids, a single instance only excepted."

The excepted instance is the falls in the Ohio. They are opposite Louisville, Kentucky, 604.5 miles downstream from Pittsburgh. There the river is almost a mile wide. In Jefferson's day, they consisted of rock reefs. Instead of these reefs extending across the river from shore to shore, they wound diagonally across it for more than two miles. It is as if some giant serpent or dinosaur had tried to cross the river but its backbone had been broken and parts were washed downstream. Thus, it died leaving a jagged, spiny backbone for the water to course over. These reefs, made of Jeffersonville limestone laid down in the Devonian era about 333,000,000 years ago, formed foaming rapids of almost three miles tumbling down an elevation of about twenty-six feet. In the right water conditions, shallow draft vessels could, with daring skippers, take a chance shooting the rapids downstream, but a costly and time-consuming portage was always necessary coming back, as shown on an early map of the falls on the next page.

Hovey realized there were three main prerequisites to be met before building a canal around the falls. The first was assembling backers capable of furnishing the capital necessary to undertake such a large project. The second was obtaining

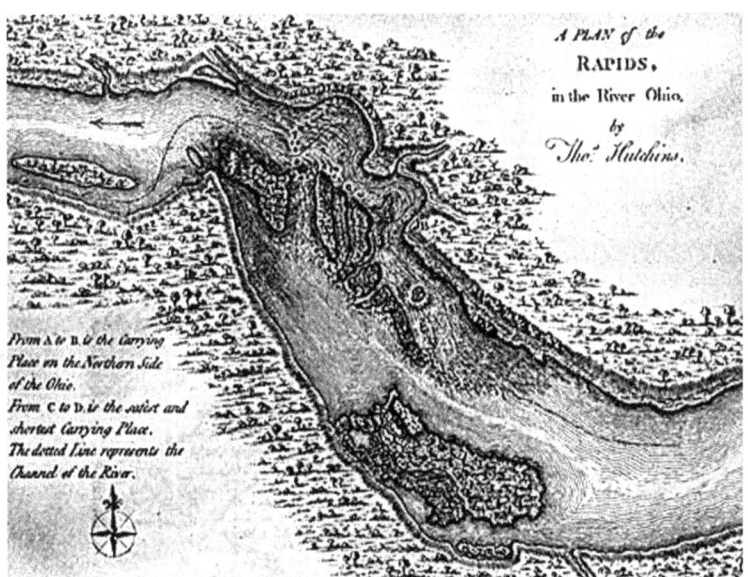

Early map of the Fallos of the Ohio River, site of Louisville, Ky. Map courtesy of Library of Congress.

political approval. The third was selecting the best route around the falls and purchasing the land. Should it be in the State of Kentucky or the Territory of Indiana? Who owned the land and what did it cost? With these questions and goals in mind, Hovey first reconnoitered the Ohio, and then sought backers.

As previously noted, the *Annals of Oxford* report that he entertained his many friends beyond "the amount his purse could bear." Some of this entertainment was in connection with twice running for the Assembly. We have no account of how much Hovey may have entertained in these election campaigns, but we do have an account of how much George Washington, a very careful record keeper, entertained in running for a seat in the Virginia House of Burgesses. In 1758, after returning from the French and Indian War, he treated his Election Day guests to 33 gallons of beer, 28.5 gallons of wine, 40 gallons of rum punch and one hogshead and one barrel of punch, consisting of 26 gallons of best Barbados rum and 12 pounds of refined sugar.

One of Hovey's early entertainments of backers for his canal project was at Biele's Tavern in Washington, D.C. A meeting of backers was held there on January 28, 1803. At the meeting General John Paterson was appointed Chairman and James Glover, Hovey's son-in-law and right-hand man, Secretary. General Paterson, who had fought in the Battle of Monmouth, was then Congressman from the district in which Oxford was located. He had served with Hovey in the mission to quell Shay's Rebellion.

At subsequent meetings, Hovey succeeded Paterson as Chairman and Hovey and James Wilkinson were appointed to a committee charged with petitioning Congress to incorporate.

To further step two, political approval, Hovey added Aaron Burr, the Vice President of the United States to his team. While this seemed like a splendid idea at the time, just as Robert Burns had said a few years before: *The best laid schemes o' mice and men gang aft a-gley.*

Burr realized Jefferson did not wish him to continue as Vice President and consequently he had no chance of being reelected in the election of 1804. Instead he became involved in the selection of a Governor for New York and at the last minute, urged on by New York political deal makers, Melancton Smith and Marinus Willett, himself became a candidate. This was a time of great rivalry between the states of New York and Virginia for power in the new republic. On the one side were the Virginia Federalists, led by Madison, who believed in a strong central government; on the other side were the allies of George Clinton, the powerful New York Governor, who was being asked to succeed Burr as Vice President. Clinton, like President Jefferson, supported

States-Rights under the banner of the Democratic-Republican Party.

Burr's wish to become the New York Governor was anathema to fellow New York lawyer, Alexander Hamilton. Washington's former Treasury Secretary had had it in for Burr, since Burr defeated the aristocratic Philip Schuyler, Hamilton's father-in-law, in their 1791/2 contest for Senator from New York. Also, Hamilton may have suspected that Burr had an affair with Hamilton's former mistress while serving as her lawyer in her divorce from her husband.

For more than a decade Hamilton attacked Burr with malicious pamphlets, some redolent with sexual slurs, such as Burr's devotion to his daughter bordering on incest. The upshot of this conduct was the famous duel of honor at Weehawken, New Jersey, shown below.

Alexander Hamilton fights his fatal duel with
Vice President Aaron Burr.

On July 11, 1804, the Vice President fatally wounded Hamilton, who died in New York the next day. Burr's chances for political office in the United States were forever extinguished by that duel. He was at first charged with and subject to arrest for murder in both New Jersey and New York. The New Jersey charges were dismissed because Hamilton did not die there and the New York charges were eventually reduced to violating the prohibition against dueling.

Hovey was, of course, thunderstruck to learn of these events. Four months before the duel he had burned his bridges behind him by resigning his commission as Brigadier General to devote his entire attention to the Ohio canal project. An association with the Vice President was now more a liability than an asset. Hovey turned to General James Wilkinson, and asked him to go to bat for the canal project in a memorandum to Congress supporting the canal. Wilkinson had served as the Senior Officer (Commanding General) of the Army after the end of the Revolutionary War from December 1796 to 1798 and again from June 1800 to January 1812. Wilkinson was noted for his manners. They were bland, accommodating and popular, his address was easy, polite and gracious, invited approach, gave access, assured attention, cordiality and ease. By these fair terms he conciliated, by these he captivated. His early medical education was interrupted by his service in the Revolutionary War but enabled him to provide beneficial medical advice to many friends and acquaintances. He was the only General who had never won a battle nor lost a Court Martial, of which he endured three, one as claimed for being corrupt as Clothier General of the Continental Army.

Wilkinson had made several attempts to have the State of Kentucky carved out of territory claimed by the State of Virginia. His efforts finally succeeded when Kentucky became the 15th state in 1792. Wilkinson had also made a trip down the Ohio and

James Wilkinson

Mississippi to New Orleans where he met with Spanish Governor Miro and discussed the formation of a new country west of the Alleghenies with the support of Spain.

Wilkinson came through when a Senatorial Committee was established to consider the canal project. He gave a ringing endorsement and plumped for locating the canal on the Indiana, north side, not in Kentucky. In fact, on January 11, 1805, in a burst tantamount to rodomontade, Wilkinson trumpeted to a Senatorial Committee that the canal's location was central "to the most extensive, luxuriant and productive tract within the national limits, or perhaps in the universe, [it] will at first glance, decide that commercial enterprise is to find its way to this point from the ocean, and that here the primary exchange of products for imports is to take place." This out of this World exaggeration is said to be typical of Wilkinson's habit of telling his listeners what they would like to hear, no matter how far it stretched the truth.

One example of Wilkinson's bent to exaggerate relates to his own accomplishments. After the final Battle of Saratoga, October 17, 1777, he was ordered to report the victory of the Continental forces to the Continental Congress in Philadelphia. In large measure the victory was due to the attack by the left flank of the Continental forces led by General Benedict Arnold, who, despite being told not to participate in an attack, led his troops with saber waving on an end run. Eventually he received a severe leg wound and was pinned under his dead horse. Despite these heroics, when he reported to Congress, Wilkinson, then a Lieutenant Colonel, attributed the flanking maneuver to himself and not Arnold. Some writers believe this misinformation led to Arnold's bitterness and later treason.

In addition to Wilkinson's glowing endorsement of the canal project and support of the Indiana route, Hovey also put great emphasis on the superiority of the Indiana route in a communication to the Senatorial Committee. He pointed out ravines in Indiana could be used for a portion of the canal. He realized there were others that might benefit from a canal on the Kentucky side. He obtained an option to purchase the necessary land in Indiana from Samuel Gwathmey.

To attract investors, Hovey wrote a letter to the distinguished Swiss immigrant, Albert Gallatin, who had succeeded Hamilton as Secretary of the Treasury. He also petitioned Congress to grant 25,000 acres of land as an incentive for investors, or alternatively, grant them a preemption to purchase 100,000 acres on favorable credit terms at the prices publicly offered.

All of these efforts, excursions to Washington and Ohio, printing memoranda to Congress, entertaining prospective investors, cost money. Hovey had to borrow $1,500 from Jonathan Baldwin, he of the short temper, securing the loan by a mortgage on the main lot in Oxford east of the river, the lot on which Hovey's house, farm and plantation were located. On January 12, 1803, the loan was foreclosed. On May 4th at the foreclosure sale, Hovey's eldest son, Alfred, bid in the property for $1,500 and a fortnight later sold the parcel back to his father. Still scrambling to make ends meet, Hovey later sold a number of lots in the Gore to his sons-in-law Uri Tracy and James Glover for $5,000. Hovey had engaged in many hundreds of land transactions, but there was much too much of the same product for it to be profitable. This was a lesson of history that investors in the 20th century Florida land boom failed to heed. Both of the two largest Florida developers, GAC Corporation (successor by merger to Gulf American Corporation) and General Development Corporation went bankrupt — the former in 1976 and the latter in 1991.

Bailed out by his sons-in-law, Hovey turned his vigorous attention to seeking endorsement of the canal project by

Congress. The Senate appointed a committee to hear the plea. It consisted of Senators Jonathan Dayton of New Jersey, John Smith of Kentucky and John Brown of Ohio which had become a State in 1803.[77] Dayton, the Chairman, was a boyhood friend and college chum of Burr at Princeton. On January 28, 1805, the committee received and acted on an extensive memorandum from Hovey and his unnamed associates petitioning that Congress grant valuable rights to purchase federal land on completion of the canal. The committee turned down the petition on the ground that Hovey's associates, "although believed to be highly respectable in point of numbers, character and property, have not yet been regularly organized and incorporated" and accordingly a legislative measure would be "premature and improper until those necessary preliminary steps have been taken."

Hovey took the committee at its word. He had an appropriate charter drafted and with a fellow promoter, Josiah Stephens, submitted it to the Territory of Indiana for approval. The Indiana Territory had been created on July 4, 1800, by an Act of Congress. It was carved out of the Northwest Territory created in 1787 by the Continental Congress. It originally included what are now the states of Ohio, Indiana, Illinois, Michigan and Wisconsin. It was governed by William Henry Harrison, who later became famous as the victor in the Battle of Tippecanoe and as the ninth and briefest President. Harrison and the Territorial Council appointed by him granted a Charter to the Indiana Canal Company on August 24, 1805. The detailed Charter names a distinguished board of thirteen directors, including the former Vice President, Aaron Burr, and the three Senators on the committee, John Brown, Jonathan Dayton and John Smith. Also named were George Rodgers Clark, Marston G. Clark, William Croghan, Davis Floyd, John Gwathmey, John Harrison, Benjamin Hovey, Josiah Stephens and Samuel C. Vance. James

Wilkinson, who had so strongly endorsed the project before the Senate Committee, was the notable omission.

No wonder Hovey had failed to name his associates before the Senate Committee. First and foremost to grace any board in the Indiana Territory, one had to include George Rogers Clark, an elder brother of William Clark, who was then engaged in the Lewis & Clark expedition. George Rodgers Clark had headed the Kentucky Militia during the Revolutionary War. In the summer of 1778, Lieutenant Colonel Clark and an expeditionary force of 300 men reached Corn Island above the Ohio Falls and made the startling discovery that white men had been there long before them. Among the many bits of evidence were breastplates of brass bearing the Welsh Coat of Arms. This proved that the expedition of Prince Madoc that had sailed west from Wales in 1170 A.D. had reached the New World 322 years before Columbus. This also explained the unusual European-style stone fort on the island and the "White Indians" who lived in the vicinity.[78]

From Corn Island, Clark and his small band launched a campaign against the English and their Native American allies. Although he had several defeats as well as victories in this campaign, he is credited as the hero who doubled the size of the United States. This occurred in 1783, when as a result of Clark's victories, the Northwest Territories were ceded to the United States by the Treaty of Paris. However, Clark had his critics. The best known is James Wilkinson, who had accused Clark of being drunk and neglecting his duty during the Northwest Indian War. Hovey could not have Clark and Wilkinson on the same board.

Covering all his bases, Hovey had on the board not only Clark but also his cousin, Marston G. Clark, and nephew–in-law, William Croghan. In addition, there were three relatives of the Territorial Governor, William Henry Harrison. They were his son, John Harrison, his brother-in-law, Samuel C. Vance and his nephew John Gwathmey. John Gwathmey was also the son of Samuel Gwathmey, one of the owners of the land through which the canal would run. The other land owner, Davis Floyd, a prominent Freemason, was also on the board.

Benjamin Hovey, using the sweet, savory and intoxicating words of Josiah Hackett, must have been saying to himself, *figs and catnip, buttermilk and brandy*, how could I have a better board? Why this cobweb of relationships is surely the *Who's Who* of the Indiana Territory. Furthermore, with two retired and one active Senator and a retired Vice President, it is not too shabby on the national level either.

So Hovey went back to work surveying the best route with fellow director William Croghan, who also had much experience with chains, links and a transit and level. In the days before the invention of the steam shovel and backhoe, it was vital to find a route that involved the least amount of digging earth with a pick and shovel. Like the ingenious method of dropping a whole row of trees in Oxford, Hovey developed a novel way of digging a canal. The route selected began at a deep downhill ravine near the mouth of Cane Creek, a minor tributary of the Ohio River. The plan was to dam the creek forcing it to flow down the existing ravine so at to create a natural canal past the falls. The canal could then be reconnected to the Ohio River by a lock, as could the creek at the dam

Just at that time, only five weeks after the granting of the charter, William Pollard Espy, a leading meteorologist, made a tour down the Ohio and describes his view of the falls and project in a memorandum entitled *Tour in Ohio and Kentucky in 1805*, as follows:

* * *

"On the 30th September I rode into Jeffersonville, a flourishing village at the head of the rapids opposite Louisville. Here it is proposed to take out the water of the river for a contemplated canal. On the

"2nd October, I took a view of the magnificent falls of the Ohio. The rapids appear to be about a mile long. On the Indiana side where the great body of the river runs in low water, I could not discover any perpendicular falls. It was not so in the middle and southeast channels, in both of which the extent of the rapids were in a great degree contracted to two nearly perpendicular shoots of about seven feet each, over rock over which the water has little effect. At some anterior period of the channel on the northwest side, I am induced to believe was nearly similar; but the great body of water that for ages has been pouring down has gradually worn away the rocks above, thereby increasing the length of the rapid on that side, and diminishing their perpendicular fall. I have no doubt that the first break of the water here is now much higher up the river than it was originally. The beach and the whole bed of the river for two or three miles here is one continued body of limestone and petrifactions."[79] The infinite variety of the latter are equally elegant and astonishing. All kinds of roots, flowers, shells, bones, buffalo horns, buffalo dung,[80] yellow-jackets' nests, etc., are promiscuously seen in every direction on the extensive beach at low water in perfect form. I discovered and brought to my lodgings a completely formed petrified wasp's nest, with the young in it, as natural as when alive. The entire comb is preserved.

"At the lower end of the falls is the deserted village of Clarksburg, in which General [George Rodgers] Clark himself resides. I had the pleasure of seeing this celebrated warrior, at his lonely cottage situated at Clark's point. The point is situated at the upper end of the village and opposite the lower rapid,

Representation of General Clark's Cabin.

commanding a full view of the falls, particularly the zigzag channel which is only navigated in low water. The General has not taken much pains to improve this commanding and beautiful spot, having only raised a small cabin, but it is capable of being made one of the most beautiful seats in the world."

"General Clark has now become frail and rather helpless, but there are the remains of great dignity and manliness in his countenance, person and deportment, and I was struck on seeing him with (perhaps) a fancied likeness to the great and immortal Washington.

"Immediately above Clark's point, it is said the canal is to return to the river, making a distance of about two miles.

"There appears to be no doubt but that this canal will be opened. At the late session of the legislature of Indiana, a company was incorporated for the purpose on the most liberal scale. Books were opened for subscriptions while I was there which are filling rapidly. Shares in the amount of $120,000 were already subscribed by men of the first standing in the Union.

"When the canal is finished the company intend (sic) erection all kinds of water works, for which they say the place is highly calculated. From these, they say that more wealth will flow in to the coffers of the company than from the passage of vessels up and down the river. If these expectations should be realized, there remains but little doubt the falls of the Ohio will become the centre of wealth in the Western World.

"On the 3rd October, in the evening, I turned my face towards home, crossing the Ohio above the falls."

* * *

Hovey busied himself in the spring and summer of 1805 in completing plans for the route of the canal and getting the Indiana legislature to incorporate the Indiana Canal Company. In addition to naming the initial directors, the charter authorized the Company to issue 20,000 shares of $50 each ($1,000,000) and conferred on it the power to authorize and issue additional shares and after $100,000 in gold or silver shall have been received "or the value thereof in lands actually acquired in fee simple," to issue promissory notes. Such notes could be made payable to bearer and negotiable by delivery. [81] Thus, just as in the case of The Bank of the Manhattan Company, Burr could establish a Bank of the Indiana Canal Company. Some historians claim that Burr had no real interest in the canal around the falls in the Ohio. His main objective was chartering another bank.

A further favorable feature of the charter was that it exempted the Company from tax until the canal was in operation. It set forth detailed regulations for the conduct of the company's business, similar to those that today appear in corporate by-laws. It also established the rate for vessels transiting the canal, from $2 to $4 or $5 depending on size, with some exemptions. Finally, if the Company failed to complete the canal for boats drawing three feet of water by December 1, 1811, its powers ceased and became void.

What the charter did not do, is allocate 25,000 acres of western lands to the backers as Hovey had requested of the Senatorial Committee. What Hovey may not have known is that Dayton, who had retired from the Senate in 1805, already had 25,000 acres. They were located north of Cincinnati between the Big and Little Miami Rivers and that is why the Ohio City now located there is named Dayton.

Harman Blennerhassett built this magnificent mansion on Blennerhassert Island in the Ohio River. It was the site for staging Burr's Expedition and the site where his indictment charged an Act of War against the United States occurred.

CHAPTER FIFTEEN
Failure at the Falls
Triple Treason was the Reason

In 1805, while Hovey was busy getting the charter approved and surveys started, the charismatic and manipulative Aaron Burr, no longer a factor in New York politics, was floating down the Ohio and Mississippi on a very well appointed barge. Some historians assert General Wilkinson helped him to acquire such a luxurious conveyance after his estate at Richmond Hill had been foreclosed. In May he stopped off at Cincinnati to meet with ex-Senators Jonathan Dayton and John Smith. The canal project had to be a major topic of their discussions. All three would be named directors of the Canal Company. Also, in view of the Louisiana Purchase of July 4, 1803, the topic of western commerce and expansion was at the forefront of everybody's mind. Dayton had planned to join Burr for the rest of the trip, but became ill, so from Cincinnati, Burr floated down the Ohio without Dayton, successfully shooting the rapids under favorable water conditions. There is no record of his stopping to meet Hovey or view the proposed canal site. The barge carried him to Cairo, in Illinois Territory, where the Ohio joins the Mississippi. Then the Mississippi carried the barge and Burr to New Orleans. During the trip he passed lower Arkansas, where he learned about a huge parcel of land called the Bastrop property available on the beautiful Ouachita River in southern Arkansas. On the way back that autumn, he traveled on horseback up the Natchez Trace making many courtesy calls on prominent politicians such as Andrew Jackson of Tennessee. He used the canal project to lead into talk of westward expansion. In Kentucky, he visited Senator Brown at Frankfort and in Indiana he met with Governor William Henry Harrison, following a cordial letter of introduction from General Wilkinson.

For some years before his trip General Wilkinson had carried on a voluminous and friendly correspondence with Burr on many matters, including the use of rivers for commerce. For example, take this letter dated May 24, 1804, from Wilkinson to Burr:

> "You are deceived my friend with respect to the size of the rum barrel of Louisiana, the answer being 450 pounds. I am on the way & team behind, my Prayers and wishes for your prosperity and happiness — as I am _with_ or _without_ observation — in warm prospect — Your affectionate and faithful friend /s/ Wilkinson
>
> The Honbl Aaron Burr — Richmond Hill"

Both men had long considered expansion to the west. The ultimate diadem there was the gold and silver of Mexico. Compared with Mexico, the profits from a short canal were a mere bauble. By the fall of 1806, Burr had shifted his focus and resources from the canal to the Bastrop property in Louisiana. It encompassed some 350,000 acres. If war should break out with Spain, it would be a springboard for an Army of freebooters to attempt the conquest of Texas and perhaps Mexico. He believed his good friend Wilkinson, who was now Governor of most of the Louisiana Purchase Territory as well as Senior General of the Army of the United States, would join him. When asked, Wilkinson did not immediately demur. Accordingly, thinking he had Wilkinson all aboard, Burr informed his potential army of freebooters that if they could not reach him, they should carry out the orders of General Wilkinson, who was second in command.

Now the problem was money. Burr may have helped secure the subscriptions of many prominent people for the canal. But subscribing and paying up in full are as different as night and day. Subscribers often deposit as little as 5 percent of the total amount subscribed and are contractually bound to pay the balance only to the extent and in the installments provided in the subscription agreement. Thus, Burr had a ready made list of speculators before whom he could dangle a brighter jewel Bastrop and possibly the gold and silver of Mexico. Many of the subscriptions remained unfulfilled as the subscribers helped Burr finance the building of fifteen boats that could together transport 700 men down the Ohio and Mississippi.

Such a major construction program could not be kept secret. It stirred the "yellow press" of those days to speculate whether Burr intended to create a new country out of the Louisiana Territory or take Mexico. Burr prevailed on his boyhood chum Dayton to deceive the Spanish Minister to the United States that he had abandoned plans of invading Spanish Territory, but was actually planning a coup to replace Thomas Jefferson as President.

This and countless other rumors stirred by the scandal sheets of the day, resulted in Burr being charged with treason before a Grand Jury in Kentucky in the fall of 1806. Burr was ably represented by a young lawyer named Henry Clay, who had just been appointed to fill the seat of former Kentucky Senator John Adair. Adair had resigned because he was accused of being part of the Burr conspiracy. The prosecuting District Attorney could produce no witnesses who would testify to a treasonable act before either this Grand Jury or a second one impaneled in December 1806. One of the principal scandalmongers, John Wood, testified that he had completely changed his mind and now believed in fact that Burr had no plans against the Union. With the help of his counsel, Henry Clay, these unproven proceedings actually restored Burr to a modicum of respect but did not result in further subscription receipts. Hovey had expended the Company's modest sum of deposits by this time and could not go forward with the more expensive dam building, excavation and lock construction phases without further funds.

Following the Grand Jury proceedings in Ohio, another Grand Jury was empanelled in Mississippi. It also failed to indict Burr. (While many historians disagree on Burr's plans, they all agree he was a competent, indeed brilliant lawyer. Most lawyers would conclude that what Burr was really doing was what any competent lawyer would do, explore a legal way in which to conquer Mexico. It could only be done legally by freebooters if the United States and Spain went to war, as seemed likely at that time.)

Meanwhile, with Burr facing treason charges in Kentucky — and later Mississippi — Wilkinson got cold feet. If Burr could be charged with treason, so could his second in command! Wilkinson was quick to cover his tracks. He concocted a story almost as far-fetched as his claim that the Ohio canal site would be the greatest commercial site in the universe. He sent a letter dated October 22, 1806, to President Jefferson asserting that Burr had recruited 10,000 men and planned to capture New Orleans and invade Mexico.

From October 1806 on, events took on breath taking speed.

November 5, Frankfort, Kentucky: District Attorney Daveiss reads his affidavit that Burr plans war on Spain which is at peace with United States.

November 11, Natchez, Mississippi: Wilkinson warns of a dangerous conspiracy.

November 12, Frankfort, Kentucky: Burr, represented by Henry Clay, has case dismissed due to lack of witnesses.

December 2, Frankfort, Kentucky: Daveiss again asks Grand Jury to indict Burr. Grand Jury instead exonerates Burr in written statement.

December 6, Chillicothe, Ohio: President Thomas Jefferson's agent, John Graham, persuades Legislature to call out Militia to stop Burr.

Early December 1806: 12 boats laden with corn meal and pork were apprehended on the way to the expedition's assembly place, Blennerhassett Island in the Ohio River.

Events on Blennerhasset Island in the Ohio River:

December 7: Four boats arrive with fewer than 30 men.

December 10: Eleven boats are ready. Militia is stationed on Ohio shore. Mob forms vigilante party in Wood County, Virginia.

December 11, 1:00 a.m.: Boats start down river. Sunrise: vigilantes take over Island. On way Davis Floyd and more men join expedition.

December 22, Cumberland River: Burr boards two boats and heads downstream to Paducah, Kentucky where Cumberland joins Ohio River.

December 28, Burr makes speech to about 100 men of importance and great goals of mission, but states these goals will not be revealed until later.

Many of the volunteers expected for the expedition had been dissuaded by the Court proceedings and rumors. Burr's contracts for vessels to carry volunteers south allegedly to colonize the Bastrop property as a possible base for a freebooting expedition and Wilkinson's letters to Jefferson finally resulted in federal charges of treason. Burr was captured in February 1807. Also arrested were the potential freebooters in four boats carrying them down the Mississippi. On being boarded, these boats were found to contain few arms, no more than needed by farm folk in back country America, such as the Bastrop tract.

Although after a lengthy trial in Richmond, Virginia, Burr was eventually found not guilty on the charge of treason, Hovey must have felt he had been stabbed in the back more times than Brutus stabbed Julius Caesar. The first stab was by Jonathan Dayton. Instead of the 25,000 acres Hovey requested be set aside to lure backers to the canal project, Dayton had already squirreled away 25,000 acres, more than enough to have the city of Dayton, Ohio, named after him. Like Burr he was charged with treason, but unlike Burr never tried. The second was by Burr. He virtually robbed the Canal Company by diverting capital originally intended for it to the Bastrop expedition. The third was by James Wilkinson. He double crossed his friend Burr by making exaggerated charges against him in a letter to the President; this prevented Burr from giving any aid whatsoever to the construction of the canal.

If undermining a corporation of which you are a director or publicist be treason, Hovey must have felt triple treason was the reason for failure of the canal. Of course, with the reports of the total amount of the subscriptions, those few backers who had paid in full or paid an installment demanded an audit and an audit was held. The Freemason director, Davis Floyd, acted as Treasurer, and accounted for every penny he actually received. He later became Treasurer of the state of Indiana and the county adjacent to the falls is named for him.

In fact, the Indiana canal was never completed. In November 1816, a second canal company was formed in the Territory of Indiana. On December 11, 1816, the Territory of Indiana became a state. At the first session of the General Assembly of the state the charter of the second canal company, called the Ohio Canal Company, was enacted into law. Its purpose was "to cut such canal from such place above to such place below to the falls on the north west side of the river Ohio, and to erect such locks and perform such other works" as the president and majority of directors shall deem necessary. No member of the Board of Directors had served on the board of the original canal company. However, Samuel Gwathmey, the owner of the land through which the canal was to run, was named a director.

The company commenced construction, but an earthen dam broke and construction was halted. Some people from Indiana claimed it was sabotage by Kentuckians. Some Kentuckians claimed it was only muskrats. The first functioning canal around the falls in the Ohio River was not in Indiana but in Kentucky. This canal was opened on December 22, 1830. It has been superseded by the McAlpine Locks and Dam on the Kentucky side of the falls. Today vast amounts of coal, petroleum, grains and other goods pass through these locks annually and substantial amounts of electricity are generated by the "water works."

Patowmack Company logo.

Boat on the Chesapeake and Ohio Canal.

CHAPTER SIXTEEN
Canal Mania
Ahead of Their Time

Benjamin Hovey was not the only founder of a company organized to build canals to convey the rich products of the Ohio Valley to America's ports and centers of industry. George Washington tried to do this twice. He attempted to charter a company for the purpose of using the Potomac River as a basis for a canal to Ohio in 1772, but the Colony of Maryland refused to grant a charter.

After the Revolutionary War, Washington was successful in chartering the Patomack Company on May 17, 1785. The Holland Land Company invested and financed it. The Patomack Company managed to complete several diversionary canals around falls in the Potomac, but relied on the variable and uncertain water flows in the river for most of its length and went bankrupt in 1799.[82] It was superseded by the Chesapeake and Ohio Canal Company. This water way, a true canal — not merely a diversionary ditch around an obstacle — began in Georgetown and extended west only as far as Cumberland, Maryland.

Hovey's attempt to build a canal around the Ohio falls was, like Washington's efforts on the Potomac, of the diversionary kind, but as pointed out by Jefferson, in *Notes on the State of Virginia*, the Ohio provided more constant flows than the Potomac.

Hovey's failure in canal building did not deter his eldest son, Alfred. Upon graduation from the Oxford Academy, Alfred went into the construction business and formed Hovey, Ward & Company. From an early date, many persons had suggested making the Mohawk River navigable by diversionary canals. By 1816, a nephew of George Clinton, Dewitt Clinton, had been elected Governor of New York. At his urging, the New York Legislature passed a bill that provided funds to build a canal from the Hudson River to Lake Erie and Lake Champlain. Construction of the Erie Canal, popularly called Clinton's Ditch, started in 1817. Alfred's Company contracted to build and successfully completed three major portions of this canal. They included such challenging jobs as blasting through the mountain ridge at Lockport, erecting the aqueduct at Rochester and transforming part of the Cayuga Marshes (now called the Montezuma National Wildlife Refuge) into a section of the canal.

The Erie Canal was completed by "the wedding of the waters" when, after transiting the canal from Buffalo to New York City, Governor Dewitt Clinton poured a jar of water from the Great Lakes into the Atlantic Ocean on October 26, 1825. Looking for another canal project, Alfred Hovey became entranced with the blandishments of the promoter, William Hamilton Merritt, to invest in a canal that would connect Lake Erie with Lake Ontario and thus connect the Great Lakes to the Atlantic Ocean via the St. Lawrence River. He invested $10,000 to found the Welland Canal Company. As one of the most experienced and respected canal construction firms, his company was awarded the contract to make the vital inter-lake tunnel through the high bluffs on the Ontario side. The specifications for this tunnel were sixteen feet eight inches wide by sixteen feet six inches high with timber rather than masonry supports. Work commenced on November 20, 1824.

As in the case of the Ohio canal there was much controversy over the route, the size and whether the canal should be confined to a tunnel, as originally specified, or opened by a deep cut so sailing sloops could pass. Unlike the relatively level Erie Canal, the Welland had to ascend 300 feet within a few miles of Lake Ontario. The specifications and route kept changing. Instead of a tunnel, a deep cut was specified. The depth of the canal was increased to nine feet six inches. All these changes were very costly to Hovey, Ward & Company. Furthermore, as the earth was first removed from the top of the deep cut there were left stable earth banks, but near its bottom the company ran into a layer of unstable sand. Water washed the sand away removing firm support for the earth banks. As a result numerous repairs were needed and by 1827 the company was bankrupt and in breach of its contract since it could not complete the canal on time. In turn, the Welland Canal Company failed and the Canadian government took over the project and completed the canal in 1829. It was immediately a huge success, traffic exceeded the most optimistic expectations, but the Canadian government refused to pay Hovey, Ward & Company for the deep cut it had made since it had no contract with that American enterprise.

Benjamin Hovey doubtless foresaw the future growth of Oxford, New York, but not the need for a canal there. After all, one could paddle a canoe for most of the length of the Chenango River, but you cannot ship much coal in a canoe. The opening of the 97-mile Chenango Canal in 1834 provided a link between the Erie Canal and the coal fields of Pennsylvania.[83] The canal had 19 aqueducts, 52 culverts, 152 bridges and 116 locks to join the Erie Canal at Utica. Besides bringing coal north, it also provided the means to transport huge blocks of Chenango blue stone, as large as 16 tons, south and east for building many projects such as Grant's Tomb on Riverside Drive in New York City.

There is no record of Benjamin Hovey returning to Oxford after 1804. Was this because the friendship proffered by Aaron Burr, a friendship he had valued so highly, turned out to appear to be nothing more than buttered-up flattery? Burr had a record of standing by other friends such as the Collector of Customs, General John Lamb, charged with the defalcations of a dishonest employee. Did the razor-sharp contest for the Presidency so affect his mind that he had to seek control of another nation? And was Hovey heartbroken that Burr had diverted backers away from the Ohio canal project? Further, his friend and mentor, George Clinton, was no longer in New York, but was serving in his declining years as Vice President during the second term of Thomas Jefferson and also until his death on April 20, 1812, during the presidency of James Madison.

Hovey had met adversity, his falls, before: some not his own fault (the failure of his family to provide an education); some his own fault (the need to provide for an unplanned family at an early age). In each case he had overcome that adversity. He had also seen his countrymen deal with adversity (the failure of their government to provide for their representation before imposing taxes). He had helped his countrymen overcome that adversity by establishing a new nation, the United States of America. He had also seen the struggle in that nation that continues to this day. Governor Clinton and Melancton Smith had opposed a strong central government almost to the extent of preventing New York State from joining the Union. Indeed, the Constitution of New York State still contains a Bill of Rights for Local Governments.[84] Today the struggle continues between those who believe in home rule as did the colonists who threw the chests of tea into the Boston Harbor and those who believe in strong central rule.

We have found no record of his activities from the time of the canal fiasco to the time of his death. We believe it most likely that he was caught up in the Canal Mania sweeping over the Indiana Territory. We believe he set his firm chin north to Lake Erie; he was determined to create a canal!

It would be embarrassing to return home to face the many local investors in the Indiana Canal Company. So first he tried to revive interest in it. But even though an audit showed there had been no misuse of the funds actually received, the company was tarred with the same brush as Burr. Its financial officer, Davis Floyd, had been aboard the ill-starred final float down the Mississippi. He was indicted but not tried for treason. So Hovey may have turned his attention to other canals.

Many new canals were proposed and some eventually built over competing routes to connect the Ohio and hence the entire central part of the United States to Lake Michigan and Lake Erie. Capital was raised and often lost on these projects.[85] If Hovey could no longer attract capital to divert the waters of the Ohio around its falls, there were other proposals that attracted great interest.

Of the many canals proposed, the most successful was that of the Wabash and Erie Canal. It started in Evansville, Indiana, well downstream from the Ohio falls, and ran northeast to Fort Wayne; thence, down the Maumee River to join Lake Erie below Toledo in Ohio. Caught up in this Canal Mania, perhaps Hovey was surveying this very route when, in 1811, the year the charter of the Indiana Canal Company expired by its terms, it is reported he died on the shores of Lake Erie.

His death at age 53 was followed the next year by the death of Vice President George Clinton at age 73. Former Vice President Aaron Burr lasted the longest; he died in poverty on September

14, 1836, at age 80. His life, beset by tragedies, following his trial for treason, is summarized in the Epilogue.

Each of these men was a risk taker, far from content with their initial station in life. Hovey, despite his lack of education, laid out and built roads through unsettled, wilderness territory, engaged in real estate deals, and finally attempted to build a canal with no background other than Yankee ingenuity. He had helped to organize a religious society, established a town, carved out a County and, second only to his children, his proudest achievement, chartered an Academy for their education. Both his son and Grandson were chips off the old block. His son took a great risk with the deep cut for the Welland canal and his grandson sailed off for California in 1849.

George Clinton rose from a farm to lead troops in battle and govern a vast newly created State. He was .a man of firm principles, resolute and brave in the face of enemies, implacable in the pursuit of freedom for New York and finally for the United States, and forever loyal and true to his friends.

Aaron Burr, although of short stature, was gifted by a splendid education and nimble brain. He also sometimes helped out the unfortunate. But he was a man without principles, a man devoted to the promotion of himself, a man who lived beyond his means, who deserted those no longer of use to him and finally a man who would betray the United States.

Does Hovey's life warrant comparing him to the founders? He was certainly not the founding father of a nation. But he had certain traits in common with the founders. Like Washington, he regretted his lack of education. In common with Washington, Hamilton and Burr, he served in the military forces and with Washington and Burr was interested in developing canals, and profiting from the sale of western lands. A further similarity with

Washington, they entertained many friends and became adept at directing subordinates.

Washington's religious views have been subject to much controversy; he more often referred to providence than God, indicating a lack of precise theological thought. We believe Hovey's faith in a forgiving Universalist God was likely based on the sermons of Streeter or Ballou and not the result of his own precise theological thought.

Unlike Washington, Adams, Burr, Jay, Jefferson and Madison, he did not have a head start in life, such as inheriting slaves and plantations. Like Hamilton, he started life with little prospects for success. Like Jefferson, he took great pride in founding an educational institution. Like Franklin, Hovey was largely self-taught, Franklin in the printing trade and Hovey in the duties of a sheriff.

One might conclude that given the head start of all the founders save Hamilton, Hovey deserves more credit for his accomplishments than criticism for his falls. He advanced the settlement of New York State, then very much a frontier. His enterprises, both successes and failures, reflect the freedom of the yeomen from Colonial rule and with the initiatives of many others of his generation, he provided the foundation for the development of America during the next two hundred years.

Some of the tragedies of his later life are reflected in this pensive portrait of Aaron Burr in his declining years.

EPILOGUE
Trial, Exile and Tragedy
Save for the Ladies

In early February 1807, Burr was brought before a grand jury in Mississippi. After hearing the evidence, the grand jury refused to charge him. Instead it complained about the militia that had arrested him. Nevertheless, Judge Thomas Rodney continued his recognizance bond in effect. This meant it was unlawful for him to leave the state. General Wilkinson in New Orleans posted a $5,000 reward for Burr's capture. Burr decided he had better flee north. En route he was recognized by Nicholas Perkins who alerted Lieutenant Edward Gaines. Gaines caught and arrested Aaron Burr, near Lake Tensaw. Although Burr's only crime was violating the recognizance bond, Perkins knew Burr was also wanted by federal authorities, Perkins put up a $2,000 reward for taking Burr to Washington, D.C. A party of eight took him, first by horse back and later by carriage, a thousand miles as far north as Fredericksburg, Virginia, where it was alerted to turn back and deliver Burr to federal authorities for trial in Richmond.

The charge against Burr was treason. The lengthy trial in sweltering August heat was held in the commodious House of Delegates, before Chief Justice John Marshall and a jury. The

Constitution states that treason against the United States "shall consist only of levying War against them" or "adhering to their enemies, giving them Aid or Comfort." U. S. Constitution, Article III, Section 3. Burr was indicted for ordering, preparing and levying war against the United States on "Blannerhasset Island". The Indictment failed to mention his then unknown attempts to enlist foreign powers. Admittedly, he was not on Blennerhasset (as it is usually spelled) Island at the time his flotilla took off. A gardener testified that a member of the expeditionary force had pointed or waved a gun at him as he stowed it in one of the four boats being prepared to descend the Ohio River to the Mississippi.

When each of the nine lawyers, three for the prosecution and six for the defense, had finished their perorations, the jury held for the defendant. While not guilty as charged, Burr found he was still deemed guilty by most of the public, although he retained a few stout friends. There was still an action pending against him in Ohio and indictments in New Jersey and New York. In addition, he was in debt to numerous creditors. Rather than facing his adversaries, he decided to leave the United States.

Using his Mother's name, Edwards, on June 8, 1808, he boarded a packet boat in New York Harbor and set sail for England. He reached London on July 16th, and tried without success to interest English officials in his plan to wrest the Spanish colonies in North America from Spain. He correctly claimed he had been a British subject — failing to mention he had treasonously fought against the Crown. For a time he was housed by the Prevosts, relatives of his late wife. He was also entertained by various English and Scottish Lords, some of whom he persuaded to lend him money. After some time he was asked to leave England as an embarrassment to the government.

He spent nine months in Sweden, Denmark and Germany, and finally was admitted to France. There he lived hand to mouth. When he wrangled a loan, he often spent most of it on gifts for his beloved daughter, Theodosia, and was left with too little for food and lodging. At last, he obtained a passport under the name of Adolphus Arnot. He boarded the *Aurora* and sailed west across the Atlantic, reaching Boston on May 4, 1812, after four years abroad.

From Boston he caught another ship that took him to New York City. There he stayed in hiding until friends arranged immunity from arrest. Soon he learned that his grandson had died in South Carolina shortly after his return from Europe. His beloved daughter, Theodosia, who was in poor health, sailed north on the *Patriot* to see him. She brought with her a trunk load of his papers. Both were lost in a severe storm off Cape Hatteras in December 1812. Some writers maintain she was captured by pirates who were known to operate off Hatteras.

Despite these tragedies, Burr managed to resume his law practice and stave off some of his creditors. He also continued to be devastatingly attractive to women. Judge Adams, who had an opportunity to observe him, during the legal proceedings in Mississippi commented: "To the ladies he is all attention — all attention — in conversation he gazes on them with complacency and rapture, and when he addresses them, it is with that smiling affability, those capturing gestures ... those dissolving looks, that soft sweet and insinuating eloquence which takes the soul captive before it can prepare for defense. In short, he is the most perfect model of an accomplished gentleman that could be formed, even by the wanton imagination of poetry or fiction."

After the death of his wife in 1794, the most notable of many pining females was Celeste, a French woman who had come to Philadelphia. She was actually prepared for defense for she declined his offer of marriage. Burr was asserted to be the father of a newborn child any number of times. In answer to these claims he graciously replied, "When a lady does me the honor to name me as the father of her child, I trust I shall always be too gallant to show myself ungrateful for the favor." Before the days of blood testing, let alone DNA, if in doubt, why not pick the best known of multiple partners. This may apply to "Fearing Burr" born on Blenerhasset Island in 1806.

In his will, he provided for two daughters, Elizabeth and Francis Ann, who resided in separate households. There were also most likely two sons. One was said to be the son of a tavern keeper at a tavern frequented by Burr. However, he went on to a brilliant career, and exhibited such a likeness to Burr, that a keen observer, former President John Adams, believed him to be Burr's son. The other, Aaron Columbus Burr, was born in Paris by a French woman. He was sent to New York and Burr provided for his early education. He became a silversmith.

Lately the Burr Association has suggested that Burr was the father of two children born to a free household servant from Haiti during Burr's marriage to Theodosia Bartow Prevost.

Not in the best of health after a stroke, on July 1, 1833, at the age of 77, Burr married for the second time. His bride, Elizabeth Junel, was again a widow, but not a brilliant cultivated one as before. This time the lady had a very seedy past but a very prosperous present. Her first husband, a very wealthy French merchant had died the previous year. After a honeymoon excursion in a dashing yellow carriage from New York City to Hartford, Connecticut, where they were entertained by the Governor, an Edwards cousin, the marriage fell apart. As many marriages do, the cause was money. Who could spend the Junel fortune? It was terminated by divorce on the day Burr died, September 14, 1836.

He was buried in Princeton, New Jersey under a simple headstone inscribed as follows:

AARON BURR

Born February 6th, 1756
Died September 14th, 1836

A Colonel in the Army of the Revolution
Vice-President of the United States from 1801 to 1805

In conclusion of their two-volume biography of Aaron Burr, Wandell and Minnigerode point out: "He lived thirty-one years too long. After 1805, they could find nothing to inscribe on his epitaph — nothing but tragedy, and grief and suffering, and these they did not consider worth recording. It has been said that the bullet that struck Alexander Hamilton killed Aaron Burr. That is not true, he had perished already in 1801, he had been marked for destruction, and the hand that was not raised to save him was that of Thomas Jefferson."

Notes from the Chesapeake and Ohio Canal Company.

APPENDIX

I. Chapter Notes
(Endnotes)

1 **Preface**

This was written before two History Professors, Jacob Rakove of Stamford University and T. H. Breen of Northwestern University wrote extensive treatises on the bottoms up genesis of the American Revolution. Their books were *Revolutionaries* and *American Insurgents American Patriots,* respectively, both published in 2010.

2 **Introduction**
Franklin Colvin Hovey.

3 Fischer, *Paul Revere's Ride,* pp. 138/9.

CHAPTER ONE

4 There are two recent biographies of Clinton, *George Clinton, Yeoman Politician of the New Republic,* John P. Kaminski, Madison House, 1993, and *George Clinton, Master Builder of the Empire State,* John K. Lee, Syracuse University Press, 2010.

5 Perhaps the most complete is the two-volume work, *Aaron Burr,* Samuel H. Wandell and Meade Minnigerode, G.F. Putnam's Sons, 1925.

6 Letter to General George Washington, March 10, 1779.

7   They were also present at a meeting of the Commissioners of the Land Office on October 2, 1790, for completing a road "from the termination of the road to be laid out by Benjamin Hovey [the road to Fort Hill]." P. 4, Albany Gazette, January 6, 1791.

8   McEneny, *Albany, Capital City on the Hudson,* p. 14.

9   This is based on logical conjecture from the fact that Hovey became acquainted with a number of Burr's New York City friends, according to the *Annals of Oxford, New York.*

10   McEneny, op. cit., p. 14.

11   See Carmen Nigro, *History of the Half-Shell: The Story of New York City and its Oysters.*

CHAPTER TWO

12   Scholars have for years attempted to ascertain the current value of the various currencies used in Colonial times without much success, especially since paper money and gold and silver coins of like amounts frequently differed in value. As a "quick and dirty" rule of thumb multiply pounds by five to get dollars and dollars by at least forty to get current value. So a five pound passage "tween decks" across the Atlantic would cost $1,000.

13   McGuane, *The Longest Silence,* p. 54.

14   An especially clear account of the threat the Native Americans felt to their culture is set forth by Jill Lapore in *The Name of War,* Random House, 1998,

15   The name of the Nipmug tribe is also spelled Nipmuc or Nipmuck, etc.

16   Today this land is used to store hundreds of truck trailers available for rent.

17   Raphael, *Founders,* p. 33

CHAPTER THREE

18 There is no historical record of Lydia's appearance; the description of her is a composite of the appearance of several of her great-granddaughters.

19 Enslow, *Music of the American Colonies*, p. 41.

CHAPTER FOUR

20 Timothy, Chapter 3, 8-13.

21 The only available sketch of Benjamin Hovey shows his square jaw. It appears in a folder with sketches of all members of the 1798 New York Assembly.

22 John Thomas to John Adams, *Papers of John Adams, III*, Belknap Press, p. 230.

23 Washington rode tall in the saddle frequently. This was because he had hemorrhoids according to an Affidavit claiming this was the cause of his delay in testifying as a surveyor in a Court case in South Carolina. This affidavit was found by Professor Julius Goebels, the George Welwood Murray Professor of Legal History at Columbia Law School.

24 See *Rebels and Redcoats, Victory at Boston*.

25 *Rebels and Redcoats*, p. 102.

26 *Rebels and Redcoats*, p. 108.

CHAPTER FIVE

27 *Lamentations*, 3:22; the entire quote is "It is of the Lord's mercies that we are not consumed, because his compassion fail not."

28 MacCulloch, *Christianity, The First Three Thousand Years*, p. 150.

29 See *UU World*, Vol. XXV, No. 1, Spring 2011, pp. 26/7.

30 McCullough, *John Adams*, p.130.

31 *Rebels and Redcoats*, p. 154.

32 Benjamin Hovey was one of 26 Privates listed on the Company's Roster dated January 20, 1777.

33 *Continental Journal and Weekly Advertiser,* July 17. 1777.

34 See Clary, *Adopted Son.*

35 Letter, dated August 17, 1777, from General John Burgoyne to Lord George Germain, the British Secretary of State for America.

36 This was the breed preferred by George Washington's mother. Alas it is no longer extant.

37 Some sources give 1778, not 1783, as the date of Alfred's birth. However, despite the similarity of their names we have taken the most cited date of 1783 as correct. It is possible that a baby to be named Alfred was a twin of Alphena but did not survive.

CHAPTER SIX

38 The names of these chiefs were related by Mr. Parker of Indian descent to Clarence M. Roof in or about 1882.

39 Inscription, Bennington, Vermont, Museum.

40 See Roberts, Warren, *A Place in History, Chapters 1 & 2,* State University of New York Press, Albany, 2010.

41 Roberts, op. cit., Chapter 1.

42 *Time and the Valley, pp. 13-16,* Barbara Wakefield Purcell, Ed.., Time and the Valleys Museum, Grahamsville, N.Y., 2005.

43 Ancestors of the author's mother, Jennie Franklin Hovey (Frank Hovey-Roof Connell).

44 Story told by Mariette Louise Meach about her Grandmother.

45 Isenberg, *Fallen Founder,* p. 96.

46 Davis, *America's Hidden History,* p. 216.

47 McCullough, *John Adams,* p. 375.

CHAPTER SEVEN

48 See *The Daily Advertiser,* December 21, 1790, calling for proposals "from the termination of the road to be laid out by Benjamin Hovey" ... on the Chenango ... to the nearest part of Cayuga Lake."

49 The account of the first winter is based on the Archives of the Oxford Memorial Library, as remembered by Gioia C. Brock, who read them several decades ago. These Archives have since been misplaced or destroyed.

50 Galpin, *Annals of Oxford,* pp.166/7.

51 Military Minutes of the Council on Appointment, State of New York, 1783-1821, Compiled and Edited by Hugh Hastings, State Historian, Herman Noble, Chief Clerk, Vol. 1, pp. 213, 215, 216.

52 P. 4, *Catskill Packet,* April 11 1795.

53 French, J.D., Gazetteer *of the State of New York p.* 229, footnote 3, line 10.

54 A "gore" usually refers to a strip of land left over between two surveyed lots.

55 The Interstate Land Sales Full Disclosure act of 1968 is set forth in 15 U.S.C. 1701 et seq. and its regulations in 12 CFR Parts 110, 111 and 112.

56 A similar account appears in Galpin, *Annals of Oxford, New York.*

57 Two or more Companies make a Battalion.

58 Two Battalions or more make a Regiment.

59 Two Regiments make a Brigade.

60 This appears in Volume II, page 690 of Cutter's Book published in 1912 before the Library fire. Of course, the Railroad did not exist in 1792!

CHAPTER EIGHT

61 The detailed questions and answers are more fully set forth in a report of The Assembly dated December 3, 1792, reported at p. 2, *The Daily Advertiser,* New York, NY.

CHAPTER NINE

62 See p. 3 of the *Albany Centinel,* 5/31, 1799, advertising an auction of 48,000 acres of central New York land at the Tontine Coffee House in New York City.

63 Boutwell, *Some Early Settlers of Oxford Before 1800,* p. 34.

CHAPTER TEN

64 Rose, *Washington's Spies,* p. 205.

CHAPTER ELEVEN

65 In 1808 the northern half of Chenango County was made into a new County named Madison after the new President.

66 Thus did Aaron Burr appear to Judge Adams of the Supreme Territorial Court of Mississippi.

67 The Constitution, as originally enacted, provided that the President and Vice-President shall be elected as follows: "Each State shall appoint, in such Manner as the Legislature thereof may direct, a Number of Electors, equal to the whole Number of Senators and Representatives to which the State may be entitled in the Congress: but no Senator or Representative, or person holding an Office of Trust or Profit under the United States, shall be appointed an Elector."

68 Waddell and Minnigerode, *Aaron Burr,* Vol. I, p. 214.

CHAPTER TWELVE

69 Galpin, *Annals of Oxford, New York,* p. 149.

70   See Public Papers of Daniel P. Tomkins, Court Martial of Benjamin Hovey, State Historian, p. 119 et seq.

71   U.S. Constitution, Article II, Section 2.

CHAPTER THIRTEEN

72   P. 3 *Albany Centinel*, February 26, 1802.

73   See also P. 2 New York Mercantile Advertiser February 27, 1802; also P. 1, Otsego Herald (Cooperstown) March 25, 1802.

74   See p. 3 Otsego Herald, May 27, 1802.

75   The same thing happened on Okinawa in 1946. When General Partridge took command of the Island after World War II ended, he ordered the troops to parade. The troops were all waiting for the next boat home and all did their very best to keep out of step.

76   It sounds exactly like Josiah Hackett from Lyme had Lyme's Disease!

CHAPTER FOURTEEN

77   Ohio was admitted to the Union as the 18th State de facto on February 19, 1803, but not de jure until August 7, 1953, when President Eisenhower signed legislation admitting Ohio to the Union as of March 1, 1803.

78   See Dana Olson, *The Legend of Prince Madoc and the White Indians*.

79   Today mathematicians would describe some of these as fractals, buds made of smaller buds, like broccoli buds, like broccoli.

80   Buffaloes found it easiest to cross the Ohio River, just above the falls.

81   Laws of Indiana Territory, [35] An Act to Incorporate Indiana Canal Company, Section 19.

CHAPTER SIXTEEN

82 Roberts, Warren, *A Place in History,* p.233, State University of New York, 2010.

83 The best know canal for shipping coal is the Grand Canal in China, originally 1,100 miles long, built by Emperor Wang in 605 A.D.

84 New York State Constitution, Article IX, Section 1.

85 There have been many such bubbles in history. The most famous is the Dutch Tulip Mania of February 1637 and the most recent the dot com bubble of 1995—2000 both fueled by irrational exuberance.

APPENDIX II
Acknowledgements

What fun it is to be a detective; I only wish I had selected that career earlier in life. What a boring job the esteemed author of *John Adams* had, sitting down to read the thousand letters between John and Abigail. What a thrilling time I have had, discovering the one extant letter written by *Benjamin Hovey*.

I have recently had the benefit of a professional Editor, Kelli Cotesworth McLellan, someone I should have consulted in the beginning, rather than at the end. This book hopefully reflects her professional touch. Any errors in spelling, punctuation or grammar were made by me after she completed her perusal of an earlier draft.

There are many professional and amateur sleuths who deserve most of the credit and special thanks for helping discover long lost 18th and 19th Century information about Benjamin Hovey. Special thanks go to Erica Nuckles, a candidate for a Doctor of Philosophy Degree in History at the State University if New York in Albany. She has recently tied up many loose ends by delving deeply into the State Archives.

If put in alphabetical order, the first of many other helpers would be Kathryn Barton of the Guernsey Memorial Library in Norwich, New York, who found not only indexed but also much other information. In Oxford, Massachusetts, Paul Brosnihan, Secretary of a Historical Society, volunteered valuable research on colonial life. From Washington, D. C., Timothy Foote, a gifted writer and Time and Life reporter and distinguished Editor at the Smithsonian Magazine, took time out from more serious concerns, to provide many valuable suggestions. The wonderful collection of Music of the American Colonies by Anne Enslow and Ridley Enslow has added a harmonious lilt to this work In Albany, New York, Coreen Hallenbeck, a skilled professional genealogist, whose name also appears in the Acknowledgements of several of the books listed in the Bibliography, found holographic road contracts in the hand of Benjamin Hovey himself and much other information. In Owego, New York, the County seat of Tioga County, Curtis Hartwig and Joan Hunt, historians and genealogy volunteers, found the record of Oxford, New York deeds, from the days before Chenango County existed. In New York City, Emma Jacobs, a History major at Columbia University, discovered the lengthy printed Communication from Benjamin Hovey, as Memorialist, to the United States Congress. Returning to Oxford, Massachusetts, Timothy Kelley, the Librarian at the Oxford Memorial Library, introduced me to many exciting materials and maps.

I am particularly pleased with the great help and new materials that Fred Lanfear, President of the Oxford, New York, Historical Society provided. He spent the better part of two days calling my attention to Oxford's history and literature. Also from Oxford, Dale B. Leach, Deputy County Clerk of Chenango County, illustrated the many changes in its borders and provided much other information. Also Joseph Titti made a special trip to Owego to obtain copies of 18th Century deeds. I am especially delighted with the special attention that Robin Surface, President of Fideli Publishing, Inc., has given to designing and suggesting several vivid illustrations for this book.

In closing, I must thank Jennie Franklin Hovey, Benjamin's great-granddaughter and Gioia C. Brock, her daughter, for their several trips to Oxford, New York, and much encouragement with this project. In addition, special thanks go to Gioia's daughter, Laura Brock, who painted the cover art which shows the falls of the Ohio River pouring off the cover of this book. Also I must thank Lawrence F. Connell, whose eagle eye caught many slips and contributed several paragraphs. Finally Jean Connell, a patient and caring spouse, told me to deep six all the fascinating details about Prince Madoc and the Welsh discovering America and a dissertation on fractals and keep on the track of the tangle of the lives of Burr, Clinton and Hovey.

This monument marks the spot of the final battle of Shays' Rebellion, in Sheffield, Massachusetts.

APPENDIX III

Bibliography

Aiken, Hugh G. J., *The Welland Canal Company*, Canadian Canal Society, St. Catherines, 1997.

Barber, John W. and Howe, Henry, *Historical Collection of the State of New York*, S. Tuttle, 1842.

Benedict, William A. and Tracy, Reverend Hiram A., *History of Sutton, 1704—1876*, Sanford & Co., 1878.

Bornemam, Walter R., *The French & Indian War*, HarperCollins, 2002.

Boutwell, Richard A., *Some Early Settlers of Oxford before 1800*, Fay Edward Faulkner, 1966.

Bremer, Francis J., *John Winthrop, America's Forgotten Founding Father*, Oxford University Press, 2003.

Chadwick, Bruce, *Triumvirate*, Sourcebooks, 2009.

Child, Hamilton, *History of Oxford, New York*, Syracuse, 1869.

Clary, David A., *Adopted Son*, Bantam Dell, 2007.

Conroy, W, *In Public Houses, Drink and Revolution of Authority in Colonial Massachusetts*, University of North Carolina Press, 1995.

Daniels, George F., *History of the Town of Oxford, Massachusetts, with Genealogies*, Published by the Author, 1892.

Davis, Kenneth C., *Americas' Hidden History*, Smithsonian Books, HarperCollins, 2008.

Elkins, Stanley & McKitrick, Eric, *The Age of Federalism*, Oxford University Press, 2003

Enslow, Anne and Ridley, *Music of the American Colonies*, Enslow Publishers, 2000.

Espy, James Pollard, *Memorandum of a Tour in Ohio and Kentucky, in 1805*, Internet.

Ferling, John, *Almost a Miracle*, Oxford University Press, Inc., 2007.

Fleming, Thomas, *The Intimate Lives of the Founding Fathers*, HarperCollins 2009.

Fischer, David Hackett, *Paul Revere's Ride*, Oxford University Press, 1994.

Freeland, Mary de Witt, *Records of Oxford, Massachusetts*, Higginson Book Company, Salem.

Gallinger, Roy, *Smoke Rings over the Valley*, Fay Edwards Faulkner, 1970.

Galpin, Henry J., *Annals of Oxford, New York*, Time Book & Job Printing House, 1906.

Grant, Bruce, *Concise Encyclopedia of the American Indian*, Wing Books, 1989.

Hastings, Hugh, *Military Minutes of the Council of Appointments of the State of New York, 1783-1821*, James B Lyon, State Printer, 1901.

Hickey, Donald R. *The War of 1812, A Forgotten Conflict*, University of Illinois Press, 1989.

Daniel Hovey Association, *The Hovey Book*, Haverhill, Mass., Press of Lewis R. Hovey, 1913.

Isenberg, Nancy, *Fallen Founder, The Life of Aaron Burr*, Viking, The Penguin Group, 2007.

Jennings, Francis, *The Creation of America, Through Revolution to Empire*, Cambridge University Press, 2000.

Kaminski, John P., *George Clinton, Yeoman Politician of the New Republic*, Madison House, 1993.

Kennedy, Roger G., *Burr, Hamilton and Jefferson*, Oxford University Press, 1999.

Klees, Emerson, *The Erie Canal in the Finger Lakes Region*, Friends of the Finger Lakes Publishing, Rochester, NY, 1996.

Kula Ron, *A Wilderness so Immense*, Knopf, 2003.

Lapore, Jill, *The Name of War*, Random House, 1998.

Lee. John K., *George Clinton, Master Builder of the Empire State*, Syracuse University Press, 2010.

Lincklaen, John, *Journals of John Lincklaen, Agent of the Holland Land Company, Travels in the years 1791 and 1792 in Pennsylvania, New York and Vermont*, Archives, Guernsey Memorial Library, Norwich, New York, G.P. Putnam's Sons, 1897.

Novak, Michael and Jana, *Washington's God*, Basic Books, 2006.

MacCulloch, Diarmaid, *Christianity, The First Three Thousand Years*, Viking, 2010.

McCullough, David, *John Adams* and *1776*, Simon & Schuster, 2001 and 2005, respectively.

MacDonald, Allan Houston, *Richard Hovey, Man & Craftsman*, Duke University Press, 1957.

McGuane, Thomas, *The Longest Silence*, Knopf, 2000.

Mc,Eneny, *Albany, Capital City on the Hudson*, American Historical Press, 2006.

Nash, Gary B. and Hodges, Graham Russell Gao, *Friends of Liberty*, Basic Books, 2008.

Raphael, Ray, *Founding Myths,* The New Press, 2004, *Founders,* The New Press, 2009.

Readers Digest, *Dailey Life in Colonial America,* Readers Digest Association, Inc., 1993.

Schiff, Stacey, *A Great Improvisation, Franklin, France and the Growth of America,* Henry Holt & Co., 2005.

Smith, James H., *History of Oxford,* D. Mason & Co., Syracuse, 1880.

Spalding, Matthew, Ed., *The Founders' Almanac,* The Heritage Foundation, 2002.

Statloff, Darren, *Hamilton, Adams and Jefferson,* Hill & Wang, 2005.

Stephenson, Michael, *Patriot Battles,* HarperCollins, 2007.

Taylor, Adam, *American Colonies,* Penguin Group, 2001.

Tompkins, Governor of New York Daniel D., *Public Records of.*

Walter, George W., *Chenango Valley Tales,* Prospect Books, 1962.

Wandell, Samuel H. and Minnegerade, Meade, *Aaron Burr,* 2 Vols., G. P. Putnam's Sons, 1925.

Wood, Gordon S, *Radicalism of the American Revolution,* Alfred a Knopf, Inc. 1991, and *Revolutionary Characters, What Made the Founders Different,* The Penguin Press, 2006.

Zinn, Howard, *A People's History of the United States,* HarperCollins, 2003.

APPENDIX IV

Chronology

1497 — John Cabot discovers North America.

1620 — Pilgrims land at Plymouth.

1635 — Puritans land in Boston.

1675-1676 — Prince Philip's War rages.

1738, June 4 — King George III born

1739, July 26 — George Clinton born in New Britain, New York.

1756, February 6 — Aaron Burr (AB) born in Newark, New Jersey, second child of Aaron Burr, Sr., a Yale graduate and President of the College of New Jersey (now Princeton) and Esther Edwards Burr, daughter of the noted theologian, Jonathan Edwards.

1758, March 12 — Benjamin Hovey (BH) born in Sutton, now part of Oxford, Massachusetts; son and eighth child of Daniel Hovey, a cooper, and Ruth Tyler Hovey.

April 28 — James Monroe born in Virginia, son of well off planter. Studied at College of William and Mary.

1760 — George III, at age 22, becomes King of England on death of his grandfather, King George II.

1762, July 9 — Catherine II (the Great) seizes power in Russia from her husband Czar Peter II.

1763, February 10 — Treaty of Paris concludes French and Indian War, ceding much of North America to England

1765, May — News of Stamp Act reaches Massachusetts Bay Colony.

1770, March 3 — Boston Massacre.

1772 — Committees of Correspondence appointed in all thirteen American Colonies.

1773 — Boston Tea Party.

1774 — Intolerable Acts passed by British Parliament. Whigs close Courts in Worcester; all Massachusetts Bay Colony under self-rule except in Boston. First Continental Congress meets in Philadelphia.

1775, April 18 — "Listen, my children and you shall hear Of the midnight ride of Paul Revere, On the eighteenth of April, in Seventy-five, Hardly a man is now alive Who remembers that day and year." Longfellow.

1775, April 19 — BH answers first call of Paul Revere.

October 24 — BH marries Lydia Haven, daughter of John and Susanna Haven of Sutton. December 8 – Ruth is born to BH and Lydia. December 9 – BH marches to Boston.

1775, December 10 — British and Hessian Troops land on Conanicut Island in Narragansett Bay and burn homes.

1776, July 4 — Independence declared.

1776, December 7 — British Fleet occupies Newport, RI.

1777, January 20 — BH serves with Fifth Massachusetts Regiment in Rhode Island.

July 30 — George Clinton elected Governor of New York for first of six terms ended July 1, 1795.

1778, January 22 — Alphena is born to BH and Lydia.

1778, Newport is garrisoned by 6,700 Redcats under Robert Pigot. Storm scatters French Fleet and General Sullivan abandons retaking Newport.

1780, June 6 — Town of Sutton appoints Moses Hovey and John Gould to Committee to procure 36 soldiers.

August 16 — Moses Hovey appointed to committee to procure 17,520 pounds of beef for Army.

December 18 — Captain Chase and Moses Hovey appointed to committee to requisition 33,640 Pounds of beef for Army and 50,146 pounds is appropriated to pay for them.

1781— Sutton appoints Moses Hovey to Committee of Safety. The Articles of Confederation adopted by Continental Congress.

1783 — Alfred is born to BH and Lydia.

1784 — Nancy is born to BH and Lydia. AB elected to New York Assembly.

1785 — New York State (NYS) purchases Town of Fayette and other lands from Oneida and Tuscarora Indians.

1786 — Daniel Shays, a farmer and unpaid revolutionary war soldier, facing imprisonment for debt, rebels and organizes rebellion. BH commissioned a Lieutenant in private Militia organized by Massachusetts Governor to quell Shay's Rebellion. Marches to Springfield under General Lincoln in January and February, 1787

1787 — Mary is born to BH and Lydia.

1788 — Constitution of the United States of America (USA) is ratified.

1789 — George Washington elected President of USA; John Adams Vice President. Congress proposes Bill of Rights. George Clinton elected Governor of NYS.

1789/90 — BH moves to the Susquehanna River in New York State four miles west of Wattle's Ferry (near present Village of Unadilla).

1790 — BH builds log cabin and settles in Oxford, NY on Chenango River.

1791, November — BH brings family to Oxford, N.Y. December – Bill of Rights goes into effect.

1792, March 3 — Council of Appointments — Militia of Tioga County arranged into one regiment and two battalions — Hovey appointed Major Commandment of one battalion.

1792 — George Clinton runs for re-election as Governor against John Jay. In extremely close election, votes from Clinton, Otsego and Tioga Counties are suspect. Tioga's County Sheriff deputizes Benjamin Hovey to carry the Tioga Ballot boxes to NY City, but BH became ill on the 300-mile trip to the City and entrusted the ballots to his clerk. Theodore Burr settles in Oxford, NY.

1792 –1797 — AB serves as Senator from NYS to Congress

1793 — Hovey farm annexed by Oxford, MA.

1793 — Township of Oxford established. Governor George Clinton reforms Battalion of NYS Militia in that part of Tioga County for those residing east of the Chenango River and its Tioughnioga branch north of the Town of Chenango into a Regiment with Lt. Col. BH Commandant.

1793, August 28 — Ruth Hovey marries Uri Tracy.

1794, January 24 — The first Town meeting held at home of BH. He becomes Town Supervisor. NYS Regents grant charter to Oxford Academy (the "Academy") the fourth such charter granted in western NYS. In October Academy appoints BH, Uri Tracy and Solomon Martin as a committee to recruit a teacher. Academy also requests BH attend the Regency of the University relative to the future support of this encorporation (sic).

1795 — BH appointed Pound Master of Town. On April 5th Sophia Tracy, first grandchild of BH, was born. There are now 150 heads of families in Oxford, NY.

1796 — Jonathan Forman moves from New Jersey to Cazenovia, New York. He is a Brigadier General of the New York militia and is elected to NYS Assembly.

1798 — BH and AB elected to NYS Assembly.

1799 — Second building for Academy erected. Among Town expenses of $331.13 is $20 bounty for killing wolves.

1800 — Thomas Jefferson and AB wind up in a tie for President, until on the 37th vote in the House of Representatives in February 1801 Jefferson becomes President and AB Vice President.

1801 — Lt. Col. BH is removed from office by Court Martial for disobeying orders of Commander In Chief (the Governor, John Jay) dated April 1, 1801, on Charges brought by Brigadier General Jonathan Foreman. December 16, 1801, on appeal to the Commander in Chief, the action of the Court Martial is annulled by the new Governor, George Clinton.

1802 — Commander in Chief appoints BH a Brigadier General vice Brigadier Jonathan Foreman who is removed from office.

1803, April 3 — USA buys 530,000,000 acres for less than three cents per acre from France (the Louisiana Purchase).

1803 — Samuel Kingsbury and Ebenezer Lyon resign their commissions assigning as a reason they animadvert the proceedings of the Governor in disaffirming the Court Martial of BH. Commander in Chief annuls their resignations and removes them from office.

1804, March 9 — BH resigns as Brigadier General of Militia in Chenango County. BH goes to Ohio.

1804, July 11 — AB fatally wounds Alexander Hamilton in duel at Weehawken, New Jersey.

1805 — AB sets off down the Ohio from Pittsburgh, Meets General James Wilkinson on way to New Orleans.

1806 — Kentucky Grand Jury fails to indict AB for treason.

1807 — AB captured and Chief Justice John Marshall finds enough evidence to try AB on charges of conspiring to invade a nation at peace with USA. The Jury finds AB not proved to be guilty.

1811 — BH is reported to have died on shores of Lake Erie.

1812, April 20 — Vice President Clinton dies in office.

1836 — AB dies on Staten Island.

APPENDIX V
Cast of Characters

John Adams (1735-1826) Graduated from Harvard College in 1755. Practiced law. Married Abigail Amelia Smith. Fathered John Quincy Adams and four other children. Delegate to Continental Congress and Constitutional Convention. Believed in strong federal government. With Franklin and Jay negotiated peace in 1783. Vice President under Washington and President, 1797-1801.

Aaron Burr (1756-1836) Son of President of Princeton (then New Jersey) College and grandson through mother of Jonathan Edwards. Became orphan when 3, rose to Colonel in Revolutionary War, then studied law. In NYS Assembly 1784/5 and with Benjamin Hovey 1798/9, NYS Attorney General 1789/91, US Senator 1791/97, US Vice President 1801/05. Fatally wounded Alexander Hamilton in duel July 11, 1804. Acquitted of Treason in September 1807, Burr goes to Europe for four years, then returns to practice law in US.

George Clinton (1739-1812) Born in Little Britain, Orange County, New York in 1739. Studied law; member of Continental Congress, Brigadier General of Militia. Governor of New York, 1777-1795, when he retired due to severe rheumatism. In 1792 bitterly fought race for Governor against John Jay had Benjamin Hovey deputed a Deputy Sheriff to carry ballots from Tioga County to New York City, but Hovey became ill on 300 mile trip and his clerk delivered them. In 1804 elected Vice President succeeding Aaron Burr as States Right Democrat under Jefferson and in 1808 under Madison. Died in office, 1812. Reburied in Kingston, NY in 1908.

Benjamin Franklin (1706–1790) Learned printing trade in Boston from older brother, but after dispute moved to Philadelphia where he opened his own print shop. In 1732 issued *Poor Richard's Almanac*. Experiments with electricity, invents Franklin stove and glass armonica. From 1757 forward represents American interests in England and France in many capacities until 1785 when he returns to Philadelphia.

Alexander Hamilton (1755 or 1757–1804) Born in Nevis, British West Indies in 1755 or 1757, of a woman accused of adultery and whoredom by a former husband and an unmarried younger son of the Hamilton family of Scotland. He was brilliant and clerked for a merchant, coming to New York City in the colonies when 16. Attended King's (Columbia) College. From New York militia promoted to Washington's aide de camp for most of Revolutionary War. Finally fought in battle at Yorktown at end of war. A strong Federalist, became first Secretary of the Treasury under Washington. Strongly opposed Burr's political aspirations, especially after Burr defeated Hamilton's father-in-law, Philip Schuyler, in bid for US Senate seat from New York in 1791. For 12 years opposed Burr, to almost manic extremes. Accused Burr of despicable conduct at dinner party (Biographers suggest incest or gay) but would not say so. Burr challenged him to a duel. He died in New York City one day after being mortally wounded by Burr at Weehawken, New Jersey on July 11, 1804.

John Jay (1745–1829) King's College graduate and lawyer. Refused to sign Declaration of Independence. Chief Justice of NYS 1772, President Continental Congress 1778, Minister to: Spain 1779, negotiated Peace Treaty with Britain 1782, Foreign Secretary 1784, Federalist papers 1788, Chief Justice Supreme Court 1780, defeated by Clinton as Governor of New York 1792, Jay Treaty 1794, Governor New York 1797-1801.

Thomas Jefferson (1743–1825) Inherited plantations and 200 slaves from parents. Graduated from William & Mary College in 1762 and practiced law. Drafted Declaration of Independence. Wrote *Notes of the State of Virginia*. Served as Secretary of State under Washington in

1790. President from 1801 to 1809, purchased Louisiana Territory in 1803 and organized Lewis & Clark Expedition. Donated his Library to found the Library of Congress. Founded the University of Virginia.

James Kent (1763–1847) Yale graduate and Poughkeepsie, then New York City Lawyer, Justice of Supreme Court, in 1804 Chief Justice, first Professor of Law at Columbia College.

James Madison (1751–1836) Graduated from Princeton, in 1771. Studied and practiced law. With Hamilton and Jay, author of *Federalist Papers*. Member of Continental Congress and Constitutional Convention, primary drafter of Constitution and helped frame Bill of Rights, but opposed to Hamilton. Changed from strong Federalist to Democratic-Republican. Secretary of State under Jefferson and President 1809-1817.

James Monroe (1758–1831) Heir at 16 of well off Virginia Planters. Studied at William & Mary but left to serve in Continental Army. Fought in battle of Trenton and Monmouth. Rose to Major. Studied law under Jefferson. Served in Continental Congress. Negotiated Louisiana Purchase. Elected President in 1816 and served two terms; responsible for Missouri Compromise and Monroe Doctrine.

Melancton Smith (1724–1798) Staunch anti –federalist and supporter of George Clinton, he debated Hamilton at New York Convention on ratification of federal Constitution but after New Hampshire and Virginia ratified it, switched sides, He was sheriff of Duchess County at adoption of NYS Constitution, canvassed the State for Clinton in 1792 election and appointed Circuit Judge. Chancellor Kent said Smith was noted "for his love of reading, tenacious memory, powerful intellect and for the metaphysical and logical discussion of which he was master." He was co-owner of some lands with Benjamin Hovey.

George Washington (1732–1799) Tutored in mathematics, surveying and the classics. His father died when he was eleven and his older brother took him in but died so he ultimately inherited a large estate along the Potomac, now Alexandria, Virginia. He served in and was defeated in battle in the French and Indian War. In 1759 he married the wealthy widow, Martha Custis. He was a delegate to the first and second Continental Congresses. He was chosen as the Commander of the Continental Army. He was out maneuvered by British General Howe and strove to avoid major encounters. Finally, with great help from the French Fleet and troops defeated Cornwallis at Yorktown. Retired to Mount Vernon, but attended Constitutional Convention in Philadelphia and supported strong central government. Elected President in 1789 he served two terms to March 1797, when he retired again to Mount Vernon where he died on December 14, 1799.

James Wilkinson (1757–1825) He was a Revolutionary War Officer and the senior officer of the U.S. Army from 1796 to 1798, and 1800 to 1812 despite suspicion of having been party to a cabal to replace Washington with Gates and corruption as Clothier General to the Army. First Governor of Louisiana Territory 1805–1807. He promoted statehood for Kentucky or forming an independent state and in 1804 and 1805 communicated with Burr about a plan for a separate Louisiana and Mexico. He testified against Burr in Burr's trial for treason. He was thrice subject to Court Martial proceedings, first as Clothier General, second in connection with Burr's trial, and finally by President Monroe but never convicted. In 1854, 29 years after his death, the publication of memoirs by the Spanish Governor, Miro, of New Orleans revealed he was a paid informer for and had sworn allegiance to King Carlos III of Spain. He had been forced to agree to do so in order to trade with New Orleans.

Marinus Willett (1740–1830) He was raised on his father's farm in Jamaica, now part of the Borough of Queens in New York City. He did not like farming and moved to the City where he became a skilled cabinet maker as mentioned on page 6. There he was also active in the Son's of the Revolution. In June 1775 he became a Lt. Colonel in the 3rd New York Regiment in the Continental Army. Willett was instrumental in bringing help to the besieged Fort Stanwix, thus stopping the threat from the West and leading to Gates victory at Saratoga. He was married three times and raised five children. After the war, he served as Sheriff of New York City and was appointed Mayor for a short time.

APPENDIX VI
Index

Adair, John, 145
Adams, Abigail (wife of John), 5
Adams, Abigail (wife of William
   Stephens Smith), 75
Adams, John, vii, xi, xv, 5, 32, 41,
   60, 75, 85, 110, 111, 116, 162,
   167, 168, 173, 179, 183, 187,
   191
   Treatise, 62
Adams, Samuel, 19
Andre, Major, 97
Arnold, Benedict, 97, 134
Balcom, Francis, 64, 71
Baldwin, Jonathan, 95, 135
Ballou, Hosea, 41, 157
Barton, William, 44
Baites, David and Molly, 65, 85
Bayard, James, 110, 111
Bigelow, Thomas, 20
Blackman, Elijah, 66, 67
Bowdoin, James, 61
Boutwell, Roland A., 66
Brown, John, 135, 136, 157
Brutus, 148
Burgoyne, John, 46, 51-53, 55, 78,
   168
Burns, Robert, 130

Burr, Aaron,
   Assembly, 103, 105, 106, 108
   Birth,
   Canal, 136, 141
   Children of, 162, 163
   Death, 163
   Description, 2, 5, 161
   Education, 2
   Exile, 160, 161
   Land deals, 57, 58, 85
   Richmond Hill, 4, 5
   Trial, 148, 159, 160
   Vice President, 109, 110, 130
Burr, Theodore, 95
Burr, Theodosia (Prevost), 3
Burr, Theodosia (Alston), 3, 5, 109,
   131
Caesar, Julius, 148
Calvin, John, 23
Cazenove, Theopile, 76
Chandler, Gardner, 23, 46, 49
Christ, Jesus, 23
Clark, Marston G., 136
Clark, George Rodgers, 136-37,
   139
Clark, William, 136
Clay, Henry, 116, 145-147

Clinton, Dewitt, 152
Clinton, George, vii, viii, x, xiv, xv,
    1, 3, 6, 7, 48, 49, 56, 78, 80, 83,
    86, 110, 115, 120, 130, 152,
    154-156, 165, 179, 181, 183-
    185, 187, 189
    Governor, 1, 3, 6, 78, 80, 83
    youth, 49-51
    trip with Washington, 55, 71,
Clinton, Henry, 34, 42, 52
Clinton, James, 52, 55
Columbus, 137, 162
Cooper, James Fennimore, 100
Croghan, William, 136-138
Davis, Hovey, 40
Davis, Kenneth C., 60
Dayton, Jonathan, 135, 136, 143, 148
D'Estaing, Charles-Henry-Theodat, 45
Dodge, Solomon, 64, 69, 71
Dudley, Joseph, 14
Dwight, Timothy, 120
Edwards, Jonathan, 2, 57, 58, 181, 187
Edwards, Jonathan, Jr., 57
Edwards, Timothy, 2, 57-58
Edwards, Pierpont, 57
Eliot, John, 11
Espy, William Pollard, 138
Fischer, David Hackett, x
Fish, Luman, 125
Floyd, Davis, 136, 137, 147, 149, 155
Forman, Jonathan, 114, 115, 118, 119, 121, 185
Franklin, Benjamin, vii, xv, 60, 188
Gallatin, Albert, 134
Gates, Horatio, 53, 55
Glover, James A., 80

Glover, James, xiv, 80, 101, 115, 130, 135
Grant, U. S., 154
Green, Elizabeth, 22
Gwathmey, John, 136, 137, 192
Gwathmey, Samuel, 134, 137, 149
Hackett, Josiah, 34, 121, 125, 137, 171
Hadley, David, 60
Hamilton, Alexander, vii, xv, 2, 62, 77, 109, 110, 131, 163, 185, 187, 188
Harrison, John, 136, 137
Harrison, William Henry, 136, 137, 144
Hauptman, Rick & Russell, 102
Haven, John, 14, 23, 26
Haven, Susanna, 26
Haven, Lydia (Hovey), 23, 26, 28
Holman, Jonathan, 43, 44
Hopkins, Samuel Miles, 84
Hovey, Alfred, 152
Hovey, Alphena, xiv, 80, 102, 115
Hovey, Anna, 13
Hovey, Benjamin,
    Appointed Major, 3, 71; Lt. Col., 86
    Birth, 17
    Builds roads, 63-65, contract 72, 73
    Canal Company, 127-144
    Deputy Sheriff, 59
    Founds Academy, 97-99
    Hackett story, 122-126
    Heads west, 127, 128
    Marriage, 25
    Shay's Rebellion, 36
    Trial, 113-117
    Religion, 40, 41
    Supervisor, 103

Hovey, Daniel, #1, 7, 9
Hovey, Daniel, III, 12-14
Hovey, Daniel, # 4, 22
Hovey, Franklin Colvin, 100, 165
Hovey, John Tyler, 22
Hovey, Joshua, 13, 22
Hovey, Mary, 22, 63
Hovey, Moses, 21, 22, 88
Hovey, Nancy, 60
Hovey, Otis, 102
Hovey, Ruth (Tracy), 26
Hovey, Thomas, 22
Hovey, Samuel, 69
Howe, George, 43
Howe, Richard, 43
Howe, William, 33, 37-39, 43. 52
Hubbard, Everett S., 10
Hutchinson, Thomas, 19
Hyde, Caleb, 103
Hyde, Edward, Viscount Cornbury, 50
Hyde, W. H., 99
Isenberg, Nancy, 57
Jackson, Andrew, 144
Jay, John, vii, xv, 60, 62, 87, 114, 115, 119, 184, 185, 187, 188
Jefferson, Thomas, vii, xiv, xv, 2, 110-112, 128, 145, 147, 154, 163, 185, 188
Junel, Elizabeth, 162
Kent, James, xv, 123, 189
King George II, 3
King George III, xiv, 18, 38, 181
King Louis XIV, 13
King Philip (see Metacom), 11, 12
Kingsbury, Jeremiah, 44
Kingsbury, Lemuel, 120
Knox, Henry, 37
Lafayette, Marquis de, 45, 60
Lamb, John, 6, 84, 154

Latimer, James, 111
Lee, Charles, 42, 45
Le Jeune, Paul, 8
Lincoln, Benjamin, 61
Lincklaen, John, 73, 179
Locke, C.F.T., 106, 125
Locke, Nathaniel, 74, 76, 106
Lyon, Ebenezer, 120, 185
Lyons, Stephen, 86
Madison, James, xv, 2, 62, 154, 189
Massasoit, 10, 11
McAlpine, Thomas and James, 64
Madoc, Prince, 137, 171, 175
Merritt, William Hamilton, 152
Messenger, Anne (Tyler), 13
Metacom, 11
Monroe, James, xv, 127, 181, 189
Morris, Jacob, 113
Morris, Richard B., vii
Mortimer, Abraham, 5
Mygatt, Henry R., 98-100
Napoleon, 127
Neck, Thick, 65-66
North, Frederick Lord, 118
Paine, Thomas, 40
Paterson, John, 130
Paulding, John, 97
Phelps, James, 66
Pitt, William, the Elder, 18
Prescott, Richard, 43
Prevost (Burr), Theodosia, 3
Pulteney, William, 85
Putnam, Israel, 33, 36
Putnam, Rufus, 37
Ray, Major, 115
Revere, Paul, vii, x, xi, xiv, 25, 27, 165, 178, 182
Roosevelt, James and Nicholas, 83
Schuyler, Philip, 53, 131, 188
Shattuck, Job, xiv, 60, 61

Shays, Daniel, xiv, 34, 60, 61, 183
Smith, Abigail (See Adams, John)
Smith, John, 135, 136, 143
Smith, Melancton, xiv, xv, 6, 57, 65, 77, 83, 85, 86, 130, 154, 189
Smith, Samuel, 111
Smith, William Stephens, 75, 85
Smith, Zalmon, 106
St. Ledger, Barrimore, 53, 77
St. Peter, 126
Stephens, Josiah, 136
Streeter, Adam, 40
Sullivan, John, 45, 54, 75
Thomas, John, 32, 167
Tracy, Uri, 71, 76, 84, 97-100, 106, 135, 184
Tyler, John and Ann (Messenger), 14, 22
Tyler, Ruth (Hovey), 13
Trull, John, xi

Van Cortlandt, Pierre, 86
Van Rensselaer, Philip, 87
Vance, Samuel C., 136, 137
Von Steuben, 75
Wampus, John, 14
Ward, Artemas, 31, 33
Washington, George, vii, xi, xiv, xv, 5, 17, 34, 43, 97, 113, 129, 151, 165, 168, 183, 189
Wilkinson, James, xiv, xv, 127, 130, 132, 133, 136, 137, 148, 186, 190
Willett, Marinus, xiv, 5, 6, 77-79, 83, 85, 95, 108, 130
Winthrop, John, 9, 177
Winthrop, John the Younger, 9
Wood, John, 146
Woodbury, Bartholomew, 24, 36

www.ingramcontent.com/pod-product-compliance
Lightning Source LLC
Chambersburg PA
CBHW052025070526
44584CB00016B/1912